Personal Finance Strategies

Strategies for Wealth Accumulation Your Path for Financial Independence

BrightPath Publishing

Table of Contents

Chapter 1	1
Introduction to Wealth Accumulation	1
Defining Passive Income and Its Benefits	2
Benefits of Passive Income	5
Common Sources of Passive Income	7
Overview of the Roadmap to Financial Independence	10
Importance of Mindset in Wealth Building	13
Bringing It All Together	16
Reference List	17
Chapter 2	19
Budgeting: The Foundation of Wealth	19
Creating a Sustainable Budget	20
Tracking Expenses Effectively	22
Prioritizing Financial Goals	25
Utilizing Technology in Budgeting	28
The Bottom Line	31
Reference List	32
Chapter 3	34
Understanding Passive Income Streams	34
Different Types of Passive Income Sources	35

Advantages and Disadvantages of Each Source	37
How to Choose the Right Passive Income Stream	40
Strategic Approach to Passive Income Generation	43
Final Insights	45
Reference List	46
Chapter 4	**48**
Real Estate Investment Strategies	**48**
Identifying Lucrative Real Estate Opportunities	49
Financing and Mortgage Options	52
Managing Properties for Steady Income	54
Utilizing Technology in Real Estate Investments	56
Bringing It All Together	59
Reference List	60
Chapter 5	**62**
Navigating the Stock Market	**62**
Basics of Stock Investing	63
Building a Diversified Portfolio	65
Risk Management in Stock Trading	67
Market Research and Analysis	70
Summary and Reflections	73
Reference List	74
Chapter 6	**76**
Embracing Entrepreneurship for Income Diversification	**76**

Identifying Business Opportunities	77
Balancing Entrepreneurship with Existing Income	79
Building a Brand and Online Presence	82
Evaluating and Developing Business Ideas	85
Bringing It All Together	87
Chapter 7	**89**
Retirement Planning and Early Financial Independence	**89**
Setting Retirement Goals	90
Investment Strategies for Retirement Planning	92
Transitioning to Retirement Effectively	95
Adjusting Retirement Plans Over Time	97
Concluding Thoughts	100
Reference List	101
Chapter 8	**103**
Tools and Techniques for Smart Investments	**103**
Using Technology for Financial Management	104
Analyzing Investment Opportunities	107
Understanding Market Trends	110
Leveraging Diversification for Risk Management	113
Summary and Reflections	116
Reference List	117

Chapter 9 — 119
Success Stories: Learning from the Pros — 119
- Case Studies of Financial Success — 120
- Lessons from Failures and How to Avoid Them — 122
- Adopting Strategies from Successful Investors — 125
- Diverse Paths to Wealth — 128
- Concluding Thoughts — 131
- Reference List — 132

Chapter 10 — 134
Mindset Shifts for Wealth Building — 134
- Overcoming Psychological Barriers to Wealth — 135
- Developing a Growth Mindset — 138
- Importance of Perseverance and Discipline — 141
- Embracing Failure as Learning — 143
- Insights and Implications — 146
- Reference List — 147

Chapter 11 — 149
Common Mistakes and How to Avoid Them — 149
- Recognizing Misleading Investment Opportunities — 150
- Avoiding Over-Leverage and Excessive Risk — 153
- Learning from Past Financial Mistakes — 156

Educating on Financial Safety Measures	159
Final Thoughts	162
Reference List	163
Chapter 12	**165**
Conclusion: Your Path to a Carefree Lifestyle	**165**
Recap Key Strategies and Insights	166
Creating a Personalized Action Plan	168
Encouragement to Pursue Financial Independence	170
Taking Confident Steps Forward	173
Final Thoughts	176
Reference List	177

Chapter 1

Introduction to Wealth Accumulation

Wealth accumulation through passive income is a concept that can redefine one's financial future. As individuals navigate their financial journeys, the ability to earn without active continuous work becomes an attractive proposition. Understanding such income requires a departure from traditional earning methods that demand persistent effort and time commitment. Instead, it opens the door to a financial landscape where money works independently, enhancing stability and freedom. The initial allure of passive income lies in its promise of financial liberation from conventional constraints. Yet, the path to harnessing this power is far from instantaneous. It demands an informed approach characterized by strategic diversification and patient groundwork.

In this chapter, readers will delve into the distinctions between active and passive income, setting the stage for exploring how these differences impact personal financial strategies. The examination starts with defining passive income, emphasizing why it is indispensable for those seeking to escape the grind of paycheck-to-paycheck existence. Legitimate avenues like dividends, rental properties, and intellectual property will be explored, highlighting how they contribute to financial stability and growth. The narrative will also address common myths associated with passive income, clarifying misconceptions that hinder effective use. Moreover, the discussion will extend into practical examples and scenarios illustrating the transformative potential of diversified income sources. This journey equips readers with insights necessary to shift perspectives, encouraging them to embrace passive income as an integral facet of their long-term financial plans.

Defining Passive Income and Its Benefits

The path to financial freedom is fundamentally linked with the concept of passive income, a term frequently misunderstood because of its seemingly effortless appeal. Passive income refers to the earnings accumulated from various investments and ventures that necessitate minimal active engagement once they have been established. This source of income is paramount in achieving financial freedom, providing individuals the means to escape the traditional paycheck-to-paycheck cycle and secure a more stable financial future.

To understand passive income, it's essential to grasp its distinction from active income. Active income involves direct compensation for work performed—salaries, wages, or profits from running one's business. These require daily active involvement. Passive income, however, is derived from assets such as rental properties, dividend stocks, or royalties from intellectual property, which generate income continuously without constant laborious input. For example, an individual might earn dividends by investing in stocks of companies that routinely pay out a portion of their profits to shareholders. This method provides a steady income stream after initial selection and purchase, illustrating the essence of minimal daily effort.

Recognizing the difference between these two types of income is crucial for effective financial planning. Active income binds individuals to time commitments directly proportional to earnings. Meanwhile, passive income offers the opportunity to decouple time from money, allowing one to earn consistently while focusing energy elsewhere. This decoupling contributes significantly to financial freedom by freeing up time and resources for other pursuits.

Diversifying income sources through passive means also enhances financial stability. A single job or business venture can be vulnerable to market shifts, economic downturns, or personal circumstances like illness. By cultivating multiple streams of passive income, individuals can mitigate these risks. Imagine owning rental properties across different regions; if one area experiences economic decline, properties in thriving areas help offset losses, keeping overall income stable. This diversification acts like a financial safety net, stabilizing income and protecting against unforeseen changes.

However, pursuing passive income isn't devoid of initial efforts and misunderstandings. A common misconception is viewing passive income as immediate wealth with little work involved, a notion perpetuated by media promising quick riches. In reality, substantial upfront investment is often necessary. Setting up a rental property, for instance, requires purchasing, renovating, and marketing before seeing any returns. Similarly, creating a successful online course demands time spent on research, content creation, and platform management. The journey to passive income often begins with significant groundwork, contradicting the myth of quick and effortless earnings.

Moreover, passive income does not immediately replace regular employment. It serves initially as a supplement rather than a complete substitute. Many aspiring earners misjudge its immediate impact, expecting rapid financial independence. This perspective neglects the gradual nature of building substantial passive income—one typically starts small, with potential growth over months or years. During the initial phases, maintaining a primary job ensures financial security while gradually phasing passive income streams into prominence.

These myths can deter individuals from accurately assessing passive income's role in their financial strategy. By understanding passive income as a process involving careful planning, ongoing management, and realistic expectations, aspiring earners can make informed decisions. It's important to recognize that while initial steps demand time, effort, and resources, the long-term benefits are substantial. Successfully navigating this landscape requires patience, diversified investments, and regular management to adapt to changing markets.

For young professionals eager to transition from persistent financial struggle to independence, middle-aged individuals planning for a relaxing retirement, or entrepreneurs seeking additional revenue, acknowledging the true nature and importance of passive income is fundamental. Rather than being an instant remedy for financial challenges, passive income represents a strategic approach to diversifying earnings, reducing dependency on a single income source, and ensuring financial resilience.

Benefits of Passive Income

In the journey towards financial independence, passive income plays a pivotal role. This avenue for earning holds various advantages that cater to different life stages and aspirations, making it an attractive proposition for many. One of the most alluring aspects of passive income is its potential to offer financial freedom while reducing dependence on traditional employment. For young professionals trapped in the average nine-to-five grind, envisioning a life beyond this cycle can be invigorating. Passive income provides an alternative path—one where money continues to flow without being tied to daily work hours, thus opening new avenues to explore.

Consider the story of digital entrepreneur Emily Chen, who gradually built her wealth through online courses and eBooks. By leveraging her expertise in digital marketing, she created resources that generated income even as she slept. This success allowed her to eventually transition away from her corporate job, demonstrating how passive income can relieve financial strain and offer a sense of liberation from conventional employment norms (Chen, 2003).

Passive income also introduces the flexibility to pursue personal interests and passions. This freedom is not just about leisure; it's about reallocating time to areas that genuinely matter or excite an individual. Imagine a middle-aged professional who, after years of working within a rigid schedule, finally takes up painting—a hobby shelved for decades. With a steady stream of passive income, the pressures of maintaining constant paid labor are mitigated, enabling pursuits that enrich personal fulfillment.

Furthermore, the adaptability afforded by passive income cannot be overstated. Diverse streams of passive earnings can buffer against economic fluctuations and provide a safety net during uncertain times. An example of this is found in the strategy of investing in real estate. Many investors engage in Real Estate Investment Trusts (REITs) or own rental properties, enjoying regular rental income without the exhaustive requirements of full-time management. Such arrangements not only support a diversified financial portfolio but also contribute consistently towards long-term wealth accumulation (Campbell & Matthews, 2024).

Speaking of accumulation, passive income's role in building sustained wealth is both critical and transformative. Unlike active income, which requires ongoing effort and attention, passive income can create exponential growth over time. This is largely due to the compounding nature of investments and other passive income streams. Consider dividend-paying stocks or index funds, which reinvest earnings to generate steadily increasing returns. As these continue to grow, they bolster a robust financial foundation upon which greater wealth can be constructed—a crucial aspect for those planning retirement or seeking to cultivate a legacy.

Moreover, successful strategies worldwide exemplify the power of passive income. In Japan, popular YouTuber Hiroshi Yamazaki turned his passion for travel into lucrative content creation. His monetized platform generates significant ad revenue and sponsorship deals, allowing him to venture globally while earning passively. Similarly, in Germany, software engineer Klaus Schmidt developed an app for budget tracking. Through subscriptions and ad-based revenue, he transformed what began as a side project into a consistent income source without sacrificing his day job. These stories illustrate how creativity and innovation can transform interests or skills into monetary benefits without the constraints of persistent labor.

While the allure of passive income is undeniable, it is essential to approach it strategically. Not all passive income methods are created equal, and some require keen insights into initial investments and market dynamics. For instance, Marguerita Cheng, a respected financial advisor, warns of the inherent risks in real estate investments, such as mortgage payments and property maintenance costs, which might temporarily exceed rental incomes (Cheng, 2003). However, with sound research and careful planning, these challenges can be navigated to harness the right opportunities for generating passive streams.

Common Sources of Passive Income

Passive income is a game-changer for anyone aiming to build wealth and achieve financial freedom. There are several popular channels that individuals can explore to establish streams of passive income. One of the most familiar methods involves investing in rental properties. By purchasing real estate, you can earn consistent income through renting it out. Rental properties also have the potential for capital appreciation, adding long-term value to your investment portfolio.

Stock dividends offer another well-known avenue for generating passive income. When you invest in dividend-paying stocks, you're essentially buying a share of a company that distributes a portion of its earnings back to shareholders on a regular basis. These dividends can serve as a reliable income stream, especially if reinvested over time to benefit from compound growth. Online courses present yet another opportunity for creating passive income. If you have expertise in a particular area, you can develop and sell educational content that continues to generate revenue with minimal ongoing effort.

Understanding the varying risk levels associated with different passive income streams is crucial for informed decision-making. Real estate investments typically involve significant upfront costs and market volatility but can yield substantial returns. Stocks provide potential for both high gains and losses due to market fluctuations. Conversely, online courses require lower initial investments and have scalable earnings potential, but they demand a creative and competitive edge to attract learners.

Exploring diverse pathways empowers readers by offering flexibility tailored to individual preferences and circumstances. Factors such as available capital, time commitment, and personal skill sets should guide your choice of passive income strategies. For instance, if you're comfortable with property management and have a knack for spotting deals, real estate might be your best bet. Alternatively, those who enjoy teaching and have strong subject matter expertise could thrive by developing online courses.

Drawing inspiration from real-world success stories can further motivate and engage those considering passive income opportunities. Take, for example, the story of Lisa, a single mother who turned her passion for yoga into a thriving online course platform. Initially, she invested countless hours into recording and editing her sessions. Today, her courses reach students worldwide, providing her with a stable income that supports her family while allowing her to pursue other interests.

Similarly, consider John, an engineer who ventured into stock investments on the advice of a friend. Starting small, he focused on companies with a strong track record of paying dividends. As his portfolio grew, so did his confidence and financial security. Through patience and strategic reinvestment of dividends, John was able to diversify his income sources significantly.

When embarking on the path toward passive income, it's essential to maintain realistic expectations about the time and effort required initially. Stories of quick riches are rare; more often, a successful passive income stream develops slowly, shaped by trial, error, and adjustment. It's important to approach each strategy with care, understanding the unique dynamics and potential pitfalls involved in every option.

Incorporating practical guidelines enhances the passive income journey. Begin by assessing your financial situation, determining how much capital you can allocate without compromising essential expenses. Conduct thorough research across various passive income options, evaluating their pros and cons in alignment with your personal goals and lifestyle choices.

Remember that diversification is a key principle in financial planning. Relying on a single source of passive income carries inherent risks; spreading investments across multiple channels creates a safety net that withstands economic fluctuations. This diversified approach not only mitigates risks but also maximizes earning potential, paving the way for sustainable wealth accumulation over time.

Ultimately, the journey toward building passive income is highly personalized, influenced by individual circumstances, ambitions, and risk tolerance levels. Whether you're a young professional seeking to escape the paycheck-to-paycheck cycle, a middle-aged individual planning for retirement, or an entrepreneur expanding financial horizons, passive income offers a promising route to achieving financial independence.

Overview of the Roadmap to Financial Independence

Achieving financial independence is an aspiration that demands a clear, structured approach. This journey moves beyond merely working for a paycheck towards crafting a lifestyle where passive income supports your needs. To transition from traditional income to financial independence, it begins with strategic planning.

Strategic planning is the cornerstone of financial autonomy. It requires young professionals, middle-aged individuals, and entrepreneurs to evaluate their current financial situation critically. This involves understanding their cash flow, identifying wasteful expenditures, and setting realistic financial goals. The initial step here is defining what financial independence means personally, whether it's early retirement, traveling the world, or simply having enough to live comfortably without daily financial stress.

Once you have charted out your ambitions, identifying significant milestones becomes crucial. These markers guide your progress and offer motivation along the way. Initial savings form the foundation of these milestones. Creating an emergency fund should be one of the first targets. Having three to six months' worth of living expenses stored can protect you against unexpected life events like medical emergencies or job loss. Building this fund not only provides security but also prevents you from tapping into investment accounts prematurely, thus maintaining your long-term trajectory.

Another significant milestone on the path to financial independence is securing passive income. Passive income includes earnings from investments, real estate, or businesses that require minimal daily effort. It's important to recognize the diversity of options available—from stock dividends and rental properties to creating online courses or digital content. As you explore these opportunities, thorough research is vital. Understanding which avenues align with your interests and risk tolerance will ensure your efforts are well-placed and sustainable in the long run.

Having identified these milestones, actionable steps must be undertaken to reach them. Budgeting is paramount. A well-crafted budget acts as a roadmap, controlling spending and ensuring savings and investments are prioritized.

Personal Finance Strategies

Implementing a disciplined saving habit allows for capitalizing on compounding returns, where even modest amounts, saved consistently, can grow significantly over time. This saving strategy complements investing, which should be tailored to individual risk profiles and long-term goals. Diversifying across asset classes can mitigate risks while pursuing growth, anchoring your financial strategy in both stability and opportunity.

Exploring passive income sources should involve continuous learning. Financial markets and investment strategies are ever-evolving landscapes that require attention and adaptation. Reading books, attending workshops, and seeking guidance from financial advisors are all part of this lifelong learning process. By staying informed, you're better equipped to make decisions that positively impact your journey to financial freedom. This commitment to education not only improves your financial literacy but also builds resilience against unforeseen economic changes.

Offering multiple streams of income is a key strategy. For entrepreneurs, expanding beyond your primary business is essential. Engaging in affiliate marketing, freelancing, or even leveraging online platforms can provide flexibility and additional revenue. Middle-aged individuals might focus more on securing their retirement through diverse investments, while young professionals could explore innovative gig economy opportunities. Regardless of age or occupation, diversifying income reduces reliance on any single source, enhancing financial resilience.

Moreover, managing debt wisely cannot be overlooked. High-interest debts, such as credit card balances, should be tackled as a priority.

Developing a repayment plan that focuses on these liabilities can save immense amounts in interest payments, accelerating your debt-free timeline. Once debts are managed effectively, freed-up resources can be redirected towards savings and investments, further fueling wealth accumulation. Proper debt management also nurtures responsible financial habits, invaluable for lifelong prosperity.

It's vital to appreciate that financial independence isn't a static destination but an ongoing process. Regularly reviewing and adjusting your financial plan is non-negotiable. As life's circumstances change—whether income levels, living costs, or market conditions—so should your strategies. This adaptability ensures your plan remains aligned with current objectives, allowing for sustained progress.

Importance of Mindset in Wealth Building

A wealthy mindset plays a pivotal role in the path to financial freedom, acting as the foundation for positive decision-making and sustaining wealth accumulation over time. Adopting this mindset begins with understanding its impact on financial behaviors. A wealthy mindset encourages individuals to view money as a tool for growth rather than a source of stress or anxiety. By cultivating this perspective, you make informed choices that align with long-term goals, leading to more effective management of resources.

One of the first challenges in adopting a wealthy mindset is recognizing and addressing self-imposed barriers. Often, these barriers are rooted in subconscious beliefs formed during childhood or past experiences. For instance, someone who grew up hearing that wealth is unattainable might internalize these thoughts, leading to self-sabotaging behaviors like overspending or avoiding investment opportunities. To overcome these obstacles, it's critical to confront these beliefs head-on. Journaling can be an effective method for identifying limiting beliefs by allowing you to explore and question them. Once identified, replace these detrimental beliefs with empowering ones. For example, shift from thinking "I'll never be good with money" to "I am learning to manage my finances wisely."

Continuous improvement and adaptation are vital as the financial landscape constantly evolves due to technological advancements, economic changes, and global events. Staying informed about market trends and financial strategies is essential to adapt successfully and make sound decisions. This involves committing to lifelong learning, such as reading books, attending seminars, and networking with financially knowledgeable individuals. By staying educated, you remain agile, capable of seizing new opportunities and mitigating risks efficiently.

Success stories further illustrate the transformative power of a wealthy mindset. Consider the journey of Britt and Laurie Anne, two female investors who turned their financial situation around by changing their money mindset (*The Money Mindset Shift That Made Me a Millionaire*, 2023). Initially burdened by debt, they faced challenges like managing joint finances and dealing with the fear of confronting their financial reality. Through mindful effort, they transformed their approach, emphasizing the need to build identity-based habits that define a new financial persona. Laurie Anne, for instance, created "Luxury

Laurie," a persona who viewed money as a means of self-care, thus encouraging better financial decisions. This shift enabled them to accumulate a net worth exceeding six million dollars, underscoring the profound impact a change in mindset can have.

Similarly, the story shared by Stephen Akintayo demonstrates how altering one's mindset can lead to financial success (Akintayo, 2024). Despite initial setbacks associated with his upbringing, Akintayo adopted a belief system that emphasized the power of mindset akin to the lion's courage and the eagle's vision. His approach highlighted the significance of dreaming big and pursuing those dreams relentlessly. This mindset, coupled with actions and continuous learning, helped him achieve financial independence and empowered him to mentor aspiring entrepreneurs.

These examples highlight the importance of challenging limiting beliefs that hinder financial progress. Many people mistakenly believe that wealth and success are reserved for a select few or are too fearful of failure to take necessary risks. Overcoming these barriers requires surrounding oneself with positive influences, such as mentors and supportive peers, who can provide guidance and inspiration. Emulating successful behaviors and adopting a growth-oriented mindset can transform fear into a stepping stone for achieving financial goals.

For young professionals eager to escape the paycheck-to-paycheck cycle, adopting a wealthy mindset involves reevaluating daily spending habits and considering future investments. Middle-aged individuals planning for retirement must focus on aligning their current financial behaviors with long-term security goals. Entrepreneurs interested in expanding income streams should leverage their creative ideas into profitable ventures, guided by a mindset that embraces innovation and resilience.

Bringing It All Together

The chapter has explored the foundational concept of passive income as a key element in achieving financial freedom. By distinguishing passive income from active income, it shows how individuals can shift away from direct monetary compensation tied to time and towards continuous earnings with minimal daily effort. This transition is crucial for breaking free from the constraints of traditional employment and offers the promise of a secure financial future. With insights into various streams of passive income, such as rental properties and dividend stocks, the chapter provides strategies for diversifying finances. This diversification acts as a safety net, ensuring stability in the face of market shifts or personal challenges.

Furthermore, the text addresses common misconceptions about passive income, emphasizing that while substantial initial efforts are required, the long-term benefits are significant. Real-world examples illustrate the gradual journey toward integrating passive income streams into one's financial strategy, encouraging readers to approach this path with realistic expectations and persistence. Young professionals, middle-aged individuals, and entrepreneurs each find tailored guidance on how passive income can support their specific financial goals—from escaping the paycheck-to-paycheck cycle to securing a comfortable retirement, and expanding business ventures. Ultimately, embracing passive income represents a thoughtful approach to crafting a resilient financial portfolio and fostering independence across various stages of life.

Reference List

Adobe Express. (2024). *Realistic Passive Income: Debunking Common Myths* . Adobe.com. https://www.adobe.com/express/learn/blog/passive-income

Akintayo, S. (2024, August 12). *Council Post: How Mindset Can Influence Financial And Business Success* . Forbes. https://www.forbes.com/councils/forbesbusinesscouncil/2024/05/15/how-mindset-can-influence-financial-and-business-success/

Campbell, T., & Matthews, K. L. (2024, July 19). *Passive Income: Strategies for Financial Freedom* . Business Insider; Insider. https://www.businessinsider.com/personal-finance/investing/best-ways-to-earn-passive-income

Chen, J. (2003, November 25). *Passive Income* . Investopedia. https://www.investopedia.com/terms/p/passiveincome.asp

Financial Advisors Diddel & Diddel . (2024, April 22). Diddel & Diddel . https://www.diddel.com/blog/the-role-of-financial-planning-in-achieving-financial-independence

JessTredgold. (2023, November 15). *Financial Freedom 101: Building Your Path to Financial Independence* . Gordon Tredgold. http://new.gordontredgold.com/financial-freedom-101-building-your-path-to-financial-independence/

North, S. (2024, August 24). *11 Passive Income Ideas (And What I Learned From Trying Them) - Samantha North* . Samantha North. https://samanthanorth.com/passive-income-ideas

The Money Mindset Shift that Made Me a Millionaire . (2023). Dowjanes.com. https://www.dowjanes.com/blog/money-mindset-shift

What No One Tells You about Passive Income: Debunking Passive Income Myths . (2023). Dowjanes.com. https://www.dowjanes.com/blog/passive-income-myths

Chapter 2

Budgeting: The Foundation of Wealth

Budgeting serves as a crucial foundation for building wealth and achieving financial stability. It's not merely about tracking expenses; it's a strategic approach that involves making conscious choices to make the most of your income. Whether you're just starting your career, preparing for retirement, or running your own business, understanding how to manage your money can lead to significant financial benefits. By organizing your finances, you gain clarity on your current situation and the road ahead. This chapter emphasizes the role of budgeting in laying down the groundwork for financial success, explaining how it empowers individuals to navigate their economic landscape with foresight and precision.

The forthcoming discussion will delve into various aspects of effective budgeting practices tailored to diverse life stages and goals. Readers will explore different budgeting methods suited to their unique circumstances, such as the zero-based budget for those who prefer detailed planning or the 50/30/20 rule for a more flexible approach. The chapter also highlights the importance of adaptability in budgeting, demonstrating how adjusting to changing financial realities ensures continued effectiveness. Moreover, you'll learn about leveraging technology to enhance budgeting efficiency, simplifying the process through modern tools and apps. By examining these elements, the chapter aims to equip readers with the knowledge and confidence needed to build robust budgeting skills that foster long-term savings and financial growth.

Creating a Sustainable Budget

Establishing a solid budgeting framework is a critical step towards financial empowerment and savings growth. This practice begins with categorizing your income sources and expenditures. Defining these categories allows for better planning and provides clarity on where your money comes from and where it goes. For young professionals, this might mean identifying salary, bonuses, and side incomes, while also considering expenses like rent, utilities, and student loan repayments. Middle-aged individuals planning retirement may focus on pension plans, investments, and essential living costs. Entrepreneurs interested in multiple income streams could include business revenues and personal profits.

With clear categories established, choosing the right budgeting method becomes essential. Each method offers unique advantages and challenges; therefore, selecting one that aligns with your lifestyle and financial goals is crucial (B, 2024). Zero-based budgeting, for example, allocates every dollar of income to specific purposes, ensuring no room for unaccounted expenses. This meticulous approach fosters conscious spending and helps track each dollar, making it ideal for those who thrive on structure. However, it requires constant adjustment and detailed tracking, which might be time-consuming.

Alternatively, the 50/30/20 rule provides a more flexible framework by dividing income into needs, wants, and savings. This method can simplify budget management by minimizing the need for intricate recording while still prioritizing financial goals, offering a balanced approach without overwhelming detail (Tamplin, n.d.). For entrepreneurs juggling various income sources, or middle-aged individuals easing into retirement, this rule strikes a manageable balance between saving for the future and enjoying life in the present.

Another crucial aspect of a robust budget is its adaptability. Regular adjustments are necessary to accommodate fluctuating financial situations and prevent overspending. Life is unpredictable, and your budget should reflect that reality. Changes in income due to job shifts, market conditions affecting entrepreneurial ventures, or unexpected expenses like medical emergencies must be addressed promptly. Keeping your budget flexible ensures that it remains an effective tool rather than a restrictive burden.

Technology plays a pivotal role in modern budgeting, simplifying how we track income and expenditures. Utilizing budgeting tools and apps can significantly enhance managing financial tasks. These digital solutions range from simple budgeting spreadsheets to comprehensive apps that sync with bank accounts, offering real-time data and reminders for bill payments. For young professionals who are tech-savvy, such tools facilitate seamless financial tracking. They can analyze spending habits through visualizations and generate insights into potential savings.

Moreover, budgeting tools empower retirees by highlighting areas that require attention, like potential overspending in non-essential categories. Apps dedicated to budgeting often allow users to set financial goals and automatically allocate funds accordingly, promoting disciplined saving behaviors. By adopting these tools, individuals at any stage of life can streamline their budgeting processes, ensuring they stay aligned with their financial objectives.

Tracking Expenses Effectively

Tracking expenses is a crucial step in managing finances effectively, enabling individuals to uncover spending patterns and refine budgeting practices. It serves as the compass that guides financial decisions, helping young professionals, middle-aged individuals, and entrepreneurs alike navigate their monetary landscapes with confidence.

Exploring traditional versus digital methods provides a spectrum of options tailored to personal preferences. On one hand, traditional methods like maintaining a spreadsheet or a dedicated notebook offer a tactile, hands-on approach for those who prefer manual entry. These methods provide an opportunity to engage deeply with one's finances, fostering a stronger connection to spending habits over time. For instance, jotting down every expense at the end of the day can create a ritual that encourages mindfulness around money management.

Conversely, digital tools such as Mint, PocketGuard, and Expensify offer convenience and efficiency in the modern age. These apps automate much of the tracking process, syncing directly with bank accounts to categorize and analyze spending patterns. They help paint a comprehensive picture of financial health without the need for manual input, making it easier for busy individuals to stay on top of their financial game. Users receive alerts and summaries, allowing them to adjust spending in real time, which is particularly advantageous for those seeking immediate insights and control over their finances (Effective Expense Tracking - FasterCapital, 2024).

Evaluating the frequency of tracking—whether weekly or monthly—is essential for enhancing commitment to this practice. Weekly tracking allows individuals to catch discrepancies early and make quick adjustments before they become larger issues. For example, recognizing mid-month that dining out expenses are creeping up can lead to more home-cooked meals, preserving the budget's integrity. This regular check-in acts as a preventative measure, ensuring that financial goals remain attainable without last-minute scrambles to cut costs.

Monthly tracking, on the other hand, offers a broader view of spending patterns, providing context for seasonal fluctuations and larger expenditures. It's an ideal choice for those who prefer less frequent engagement with their finances but still want a detailed overview. This approach fits well within the rhythm of monthly bill cycles, making it easier to align expenses with income and manage cash flow efficiently. Each method has its merits, and individuals should choose based on what aligns best with their lifestyle and financial goals.

Categorizing expenses is another fundamental aspect of effective expense tracking. By dividing expenditures into categories such as housing, utilities, transportation, groceries, and entertainment, individuals gain valuable insights into where their money goes each month. Such categorization highlights areas of high-cost spending, offering opportunities to identify both necessary and discretionary expenses. For instance, if an analysis reveals a significant portion of funds going to dining out, it might prompt a reevaluation of priorities and encourage more cost-effective choices.

This system also supports the creation of a budget that accurately reflects personal values and necessary commitments. Entrepreneurs, for example, may find value in distinguishing business-related expenses from personal ones, maintaining clarity in both spheres of their financial life. Middle-aged individuals planning for retirement benefit from understanding how current spending habits impact long-term savings goals, facilitating better preparation for the future (Creating, 2024).

Periodic review sessions play a pivotal role in reinforcing accountability and promoting financial awareness. Setting aside time each week or month to reflect on expenses ensures that individuals remain engaged with their budgeting efforts. During these sessions, reviewing tracked expenses against established budgets allows for adjustments as needed, addressing overspending or reallocating resources to meet savings objectives.

These reviews are akin to financial health checkups, offering a moment to assess progress towards financial goals and align spending with evolving priorities. For young professionals eager to escape the paycheck-to-paycheck cycle, regular reflection helps build a strong foundation of financial discipline. Meanwhile, middle-aged individuals can use these sessions to fine-tune their retirement plans, making the necessary shifts to secure a comfortable future.

In essence, incorporating expense tracking into one's financial routine is about fostering conscious spending habits and empowering informed decision-making. By embracing personalized tracking methods, choosing appropriate frequencies, categorizing expenses, and committing to periodic reviews, individuals can transform their relationship with money. This proactive approach not only enhances budgeting efficacy but also lays the groundwork for achieving financial aspirations, whether that's escaping financial stress, planning for retirement, or diversifying income sources through entrepreneurial ventures.

Prioritizing Financial Goals

Setting and prioritizing financial goals is crucial for guiding your budgeting efforts. Understanding the difference between short-term and long-term goals helps create a focused financial pathway. Short-term goals might include saving for a vacation or paying off a small debt within a year. These serve as stepping stones with immediate rewards, adding motivation to continue working towards larger objectives. Long-term goals, on the other hand, could involve planning for retirement, purchasing a home, or funding your child's education. They require a sustained commitment and a strategic approach to ensure success over time (Expert Panel, 2023).

The SMART framework is an effective tool for setting clear, measurable, and achievable financial goals. This framework encourages you to specify what you want to achieve, ensuring that your goals are not too vague. Measurable goals enable you to track progress, providing clarity on how far you've come and what's left to do. Achievable goals ensure you're setting targets that challenge yet remain within reach. Relevance ensures your goals align with broader personal aspirations, such as financial stability or career progression. Lastly, time-bound goals provide deadlines, creating a sense of urgency and helping prioritize tasks (How to Set Long-Term Financial Goals [with Examples] | Yellow Cardinal Advisory Group, n.d.).

Creating an action plan bridges the gap between setting and achieving financial goals. An action plan involves breaking down each goal into smaller, manageable steps. For example, if you want to save $10,000 in two years, an action plan might include saving a specific amount each month, cutting back on unnecessary expenses, and seeking additional income sources. This structured approach transforms abstract goals into concrete actions, making them more attainable. By regularly reviewing this plan, you can stay accountable and make necessary adjustments.

Regular evaluation is vital to adapt goals to shifting circumstances. Life is dynamic, and financial situations can change due to various factors such as market conditions, changes in income, or unexpected expenses. Regularly examining your financial goals allows you to reassess their relevance and adjust accordingly. This might involve altering timelines, redefining goals, or even setting new priorities based on current needs and projections. Such flexibility ensures your financial planning remains aligned with your evolving life circumstances, enhancing your ability to achieve desired outcomes (Expert Panel, 2023).

Incorporating these principles into your budgeting strategy can significantly enhance financial management. Begin by distinguishing short-term from long-term objectives, ensuring both types of goals are addressed in your budget. Prioritize short-term goals to gain quick wins while simultaneously setting aside resources for long-term ambitions. This dual approach keeps you motivated and builds momentum toward achieving bigger financial milestones.

Next, apply the SMART framework to refine your goals. Make each goal specific, detailing precisely what you wish to accomplish. Ensure that goals are quantifiable, so you can measure progress and celebrate successes along the way. Confirm that goals are realistically achievable, pushing you towards growth without becoming discouraging. Align each goal with your life's overarching objectives to remain relevant, and set clear deadlines to keep yourself accountable.

Crafting an action plan is essential for translating goals into tangible actions. Break down each target into actionable steps, assigning timelines and responsibilities for each task. This plan should be integrated into your monthly budget to reinforce consistency and trackability. Ensure your budget reflects monthly savings targets or debt payments, thus seamlessly incorporating goal-related actions into daily financial routines.

Finally, implement a regular review process to evaluate progress and revise goals as needed. Schedule periodic assessments, perhaps quarterly or annually, to review financial achievements, analyze setbacks, and recalibrate strategies. This practice enables you to respond effectively to unexpected challenges, such as job loss or sudden medical expenses, by temporarily adjusting savings rates or reallocating funds.

Engaging with trusted financial advisors can also provide valuable insights. These professionals offer guidance, helping refine your financial plans. They bring expertise to assist you in evaluating investment strategies, tax implications, and risk management options, ensuring your goals are realistic and informed by expert advice (How to Set Long-Term Financial Goals [with Examples] | Yellow Cardinal Advisory Group, n.d.).

Young professionals, middle-aged individuals, and entrepreneurs alike can benefit greatly from applying these strategies. For young professionals, it means escaping the paycheck-to-paycheck cycle through disciplined savings and judicious spending. Middle-aged individuals can fortify their retirement plans by aligning investment strategies with retirement horizons. Entrepreneurs can diversify income streams purposefully, leveraging profits to meet both personal and business objectives.

Regardless of your stage in life, emphasizing financial goals paves the way for better budgets. It creates a roadmap, guiding all aspects of financial decision-making. With clearly defined destinations, you can confidently navigate life's uncertainties, knowing that each financial choice contributes to long-term success.

Utilizing Technology in Budgeting

In the modern world, technology plays an integral role in almost every aspect of our lives, including personal finance management. With the aim of establishing strong budgeting practices to maximize savings, leveraging technology can significantly enhance budgeting efficiency and accuracy. For those seeking financial stability or planning for retirement, employing digital tools is a game changer.

Among the plethora of budgeting apps available today, each offers unique features that simplify the budgeting process while providing real-time insights into your financial health. For instance, apps like YNAB (You Need A Budget) employ a zero-based budgeting system, helping users allocate every dollar of their income towards specific financial goals. This app not only links to your bank accounts but also works seamlessly across devices like mobile, desktop, and even smartwatches (Ayoola, 2024).

Understanding how these tools operate can transform one's approach to money management. Goodbudget utilizes a digital envelope system, reminiscent of old-school cash-based budgeting methods, while EveryDollar focuses on simple zero-based budgeting for straightforward financial planning. Empower Personal Wealth aids in tracking both wealth and spending, whereas PocketGuard provides a simplified snapshot of your budget, ensuring you never overspend. For individuals managing finances jointly with a partner, Honeydue offers collaborative budgeting features (Ayoola, 2024). Simplifi by Quicken is ideal for those seeking a balance between functionality and user-friendliness, whereas Quicken Classic allows more detailed financial oversight (*The Best Personal Finance Software for 2022*, n.d.).

In addition to simplifying processes, technology enhances accountability by incorporating reminders and alerts within these apps. They ensure that you pay bills on time, stick to your budget, and are constantly aware of upcoming financial commitments. An example is the alert feature in many apps that notifies users of any deviations from planned expenditures, thus promoting a disciplined approach to money management (Ayoola, 2024).

Digital platforms offer sophisticated expenditure analysis and trend identification capabilities, which were previously hard to achieve manually. By analyzing data over time, these tools provide valuable insights into spending patterns—helping users identify areas where they can cut costs or reallocate resources. This feature enables individuals to make informed decisions that align with their long-term financial objectives, whether it's saving for a holiday, buying a house, or preparing for retirement (*The Best Personal Finance Software for 2022*, n.d.).

Security remains a crucial consideration when using financial apps. These applications handle sensitive information, necessitating robust security measures to protect against fraud and data breaches. Many budgeting apps deploy advanced encryption technologies, two-factor authentication, and biometric security features like fingerprint recognition to safeguard personal financial data. Users should prioritize these security aspects when considering which app best suits their needs, as it ensures peace of mind that their private financial details remain secure (Ayoola, 2024).

For entrepreneurs interested in expanding their financial portfolios, understanding budgeting software's security protocols is paramount. It helps in maintaining trust and integrity, which are vital elements in business operations. A well-protected financial system not only benefits personal use but also adds credibility when managing business finances digitally (*The Best Personal Finance Software for 2022*, n.d.).

Moreover, the intuitive nature of most apps means they cater to all levels of financial literacy. Beginners can rely on guided setups and tutorials, while seasoned users benefit from customizable features, allowing for tailored financial strategies. This adaptability makes technology-inclusive budgeting an accessible and practical solution for various audiences—from young professionals breaking free from paycheck-to-paycheck living, to middle-aged individuals focusing on retirement plans (Ayoola, 2024).

The Bottom Line

Establishing strong budgeting practices can significantly impact your financial journey. This chapter has explored various methods to create a sustainable budget tailored to the unique needs of young professionals, middle-aged individuals, and entrepreneurs. By categorizing income and expenses and choosing a suitable budgeting method, you can gain clarity on your financial status and make informed decisions. Utilizing technology and budgeting tools further enhances your ability to track spending and adapt budgets to changing circumstances. These strategies lay the foundation for effective money management, whether you're escaping the paycheck-to-paycheck cycle, preparing for retirement, or expanding business ventures.

As you prioritize your financial goals, it's essential to understand the balance between short-term gratification and long-term success. Implementing the SMART framework helps in setting realistic and measurable objectives, ensuring your aspirations align with broader life goals. Crafting action plans and committing to regular evaluations reinforce accountability and allow adjustments as needed. With these strategies, you empower yourself to navigate life's uncertainties confidently, positioning yourself for a secure and prosperous future. The journey towards financial empowerment requires ongoing commitment and adaptability, but by integrating these practices, you set yourself up for lasting success.

Reference List

Ayoola, E. (2024, February 20). *The 7 Best Budget Apps for 2021* . NerdWallet. https://www.nerdwallet.com/article/finance/best-budget-apps

B, M. (2024, September 11). *Three Types of Budgets: Find the Right Fit for Your Finances* . Oneazcu.com; OneAZ Credit Union. https://www.oneazcu.com/about/financial-resources/saving-budgeting/three-types-of-budgets/

Creating, I. (2024). *The Role Of Expense Tracking In Creating A Budget - FasterCapital* . FasterCapital. https://fastercapital.com/topics/the-role-of-expense-tracking-in-creating-a-budget.html

Expert Panel. (2023, March 14). *15 Tips For Setting Realistic Financial Goals And Sticking To Them* . Forbes. https://www.forbes.com/councils/forbesfinancecouncil/2023/03/14/15-tips-for-setting-realistic-financial-goals-and-sticking-to-them/

Effective Expense Tracking - FasterCapital. (2024). *Effective Expense Tracking - FasterCapital* . FasterCapital. https://fastercapital.com/startup-topic/Effective-Expense-Tracking.html

How to Set Long-Term Financial Goals [with Examples] | Yellow Cardinal Advisory Group . (n.d.). Www.bankatfirst.com. https://www.bankatfirst.com/personal/discover/flourish/how-to-set-long-term-financial-goals.html

The Best Personal Finance Software for 2022 . (n.d.). PCMAG. https://www.pcmag.com/picks/the-best-personal-finance-services

Tamplin, T. (n.d.). *5 Common Budgeting Methods That Can Build Financial Security* . Forbes. https://www.forbes.com/sites/truetamplin/2024/03/12/5-common-budgeting-methods-that-can-build-financial-security/

Chapter 3

Understanding Passive Income Streams

Understanding passive income streams is crucial for anyone looking to establish financial security and independence. The concept of earning money with minimal ongoing effort is appealing to many, but achieving it requires an understanding of the diverse avenues available. Each passive income stream offers unique opportunities and potential challenges that must be navigated. By diving into these methods, individuals can discover how to leverage their resources effectively to build a more stable financial future. This exploration not only quenches the curiosity about how these streams function but also highlights the broader benefits they can deliver in terms of financial health and personal freedom.

This chapter delves into several types of passive income sources, presenting readers with a comprehensive overview of what is possible. From real estate rentals that promise steady income through tenant rent and property appreciation, to dividend stocks offering regular payouts without needing to sell shares, we cover various established methods. Additionally, innovative approaches like peer-to-peer lending, which cuts out traditional banking systems, are examined. For those creatively inclined, developing digital products such as e-books or online courses emerges as a viable path. We aim to equip readers with insights into each source's workings and evaluate their potential pros and cons, preparing them to make informed financial decisions. This narrative will guide young professionals toward breaking free from financial dependence, support middle-aged readers planning for retirement, and inspire entrepreneurs to diversify their income portfolios.

Different Types of Passive Income Sources

In today's world, the concept of passive income is gaining traction as individuals look for ways to build wealth and secure their financial futures without constantly exchanging time for money. Passive income streams can empower young professionals to break free from the paycheck-to-paycheck cycle, aid middle-aged individuals in planning for a comfortable retirement, and provide entrepreneurs opportunities to diversify their financial portfolios. This section explores different types of passive income streams, offering insights into how they work and their potential benefits.

Real estate rentals are one of the most recognized forms of passive income. Investing in rental properties offers not only a steady income stream through monthly rent but also the potential for long-term capital appreciation. As property values rise over time, landlords stand to gain significant equity wealth. However, becoming a successful landlord requires more than just purchasing a property and waiting for the returns. It involves actively managing rental yields, ensuring that the rent price balances attractiveness to tenants with maximizing income. Property maintenance is another crucial aspect, as keeping the premises well-maintained ensures tenant satisfaction and reduces vacancy rates. Engaging professional property managers can help ease these responsibilities, making real estate a viable option for those seeking passive income with manageable involvement. (Chen, 2003)

Dividend stocks offer another avenue for those interested in building a reliable passive income source. By investing in companies known for paying regular dividends, investors receive a portion of the company's earnings without needing to sell their shares. This approach not only provides consistent cash flow but also allows for capital growth as share prices increase over time. Dividend stocks are particularly appealing to risk-averse investors due to their relative stability compared to other stock market investments. Companies with a strong history of dividend payouts are often seen as financially robust, further reducing investment risks. The ability to reinvest dividends through dividend reinvestment plans (DRIPs) can compound gains over the long term, significantly enhancing the investor's overall returns. This strategy aligns well with those looking for a hands-off yet rewarding investment path. (Yash, 2024)

Another innovative method of generating passive income is through peer-to-peer lending. This model allows individuals to earn interest on loans made to borrowers via online platforms, essentially cutting out traditional banking institutions. Peer-to-peer lending platforms connect investors with a diverse pool of borrowers, each carrying varying levels of creditworthiness and associated risk. The platform manages the loan issuance and repayment process, while the investor focuses on selecting loans that match their risk tolerance and return expectations. The potential for earning higher-than-average interest returns makes peer-to-peer lending an attractive option; however, it does require due diligence in assessing borrower credibility to mitigate default risks. Savvy investors often spread their capital across multiple borrowers to diversify their risk, ensuring that no single default has a significant impact on total earnings.

For creative individuals or experts in specific fields, creating digital products presents a unique opportunity to generate passive income while sharing knowledge or talents. Digital products such as e-books, online courses, software applications, or stock photography can be developed once and sold repeatedly without the ongoing costs associated with physical goods. This scalability enables creators to reach a wide audience, establishing themselves as authoritative figures within lucrative niches. With the rise of digital marketplaces and platforms dedicated to digital content distribution, reaching potential customers and automating sales processes has never been easier. While the upfront work may be intensive, covering everything from content creation to marketing strategies, the eventual products can bring in revenue with minimal ongoing effort. Selling digital products allows for both creative expression and potentially unlimited income potential, especially when bundled with strategic marketing efforts.

Advantages and Disadvantages of Each Source

In the quest to build a secure financial future, understanding the pros and cons of various passive income streams is critical. This exploration offers young professionals, middle-aged individuals, and entrepreneurs an opportunity to make informed decisions on potential investments.

Real estate investment remains a popular choice for generating passive income. It holds the promise of property appreciation over time, offering not just rental income but also the possibility of capital gain upon sale. However, this avenue requires a significant initial investment, which can be a hurdle for many. Moreover, real estate markets are subject to fluctuations; economic downturns or changes in local demand can adversely impact property values and rental income. For instance, investing in properties located in areas that experience sudden economic decline may lead to prolonged vacancies or reduced rent prices. Additionally, the involvement in property management can either add to costs, if outsourced, or require time and effort if handled personally (Stanley, 2024).

Dividend stocks present another lucrative passive income stream. They offer a consistent source of revenue through regular dividends paid out by companies. These stocks provide investors a dual advantage: aside from dividend payouts, there is potential for stock price appreciation. Nonetheless, they come with risks tied to market performance. Economic downturns can lead to dividend cuts, affecting the income stream. Consider the financial crisis of 2008, when numerous companies reduced or eliminated their dividend distributions to preserve cash. Furthermore, the performance of these stocks is closely linked to company earnings, making them vulnerable to industry-specific challenges and economic slowdowns (Wride, 2022).

Peer-to-peer lending is a modern approach to earning passive income, providing attractive yields often higher than traditional bank savings rates.

Through online platforms, individuals lend money directly to borrowers, effectively acting as personal banks. Although this method enables potentially higher returns, it carries substantial risk due to borrower defaults. Such default risks necessitate thorough vetting of borrowers and consideration of their creditworthiness before lending. The security measures inherent within each platform vary, thus requiring investors to conduct diligent research to minimize potential losses associated with these loans. It's crucial to diversify across multiple loans to mitigate risk, yet even then, defaults can still diminish returns significantly (Wride, 2022).

Digital products are another burgeoning source of passive income. The creation of e-books, online courses, and other digital content allows creators to earn revenue with minimal ongoing effort once the product is developed. This model benefits from the scalability of reaching global audiences without incurring additional production costs. Nevertheless, the challenge lies in the saturated nature of the market. Standing out amongst numerous other offerings demands continuous innovation and marketing acumen. Potential creators must invest time in building a brand and establishing authority in their chosen niche to attract customers. Additionally, while upfront costs might be lower compared to physical goods, significant resources may still be required in terms of professional design, development, and marketing campaigns to ensure quality and visibility (Wride, 2022).

For young professionals hoping to break free from living paycheck to paycheck, each of these passive income streams offers distinct opportunities and challenges. Entrepreneurs seeking to broaden their income sources or retirees planning for sustained financial support must weigh these options carefully. Real estate can promise long-term wealth accumulation if one navigates market volatility judiciously, whereas dividend stocks can supplement income steadily, albeit with exposure to market vicissitudes. Peer-to-peer lending presents appealing interest rates but demands careful risk assessment, and digital products offer creative avenues for income, contingent on innovative flair and market penetration.

How to Choose the Right Passive Income Stream

Selecting the most suitable passive income stream involves understanding your preferences, skills, and available resources. Each individual's journey to financial independence is unique, and aligning potential income sources with personal abilities and interests can greatly enhance satisfaction and success.

Firstly, consider your personal interests and skills. Leveraging what you already know can not only make the process more enjoyable but also increase your chances of success. For instance, if you're passionate about photography, selling stock photos online might be a lucrative opportunity. Similarly, if you enjoy writing, self-publishing an e-book could be a beneficial venture. Recognizing and utilizing your talents ensures that your passive income pursuit feels less like work and more like an extension of your hobbies (Chen, 2003).

Moreover, understanding the initial investment requirements of various passive income streams is crucial. Different opportunities come with varying levels of financial commitment. For example, real estate investments often require substantial upfront capital due to mortgage payments, taxes, and maintenance costs, as noted by Marguerita Cheng, CEO of Blue Ocean Global Wealth (Chen, 2003). On the other hand, options like selling digital products or starting a blog may have lower initial costs but demand your time and effort to build. Evaluating your financial situation allows you to choose paths that align with your resources without straining your finances.

Another essential aspect is assessing your risk tolerance. Passive income streams each carry different levels of risk, and it's important to understand your comfort with potential losses. Investments in stocks or real estate might promise high returns, but they also involve inherent market risks. If you're risk-averse, consider safer options like bonds or high-yield savings accounts, which offer lower but more stable returns. Matching income streams with your risk tolerance ensures peace of mind during economic fluctuations (30 Passive Income Ideas to Build Wealth in 2022, n.d.).

In addition to risk assessment, analyzing current market demand for certain income streams can provide insights into their long-term viability. With economic landscapes constantly evolving, staying informed about market trends can help identify promising opportunities. For instance, the rise of renewable energy has spurred interest in solar farm leasing, while the growth of remote work has increased demand for premium online courses and digital content. Ensuring that your chosen income source aligns with these trends can significantly improve your prospects for sustained income.

Choosing a passive income stream also entails regular monitoring and adjustments. Once you've established a source, continuously evaluating its performance allows you to make necessary tweaks or shift focus if needed. This proactive approach aids in maximizing returns and adapting to changing circumstances.

For young professionals eager to escape the paycheck-to-paycheck cycle, starting small with manageable investments is advisable. As you gain experience and confidence, gradually expanding into more complex ventures can open up new avenues for income. Middle-aged individuals planning for retirement might prioritize stable and low-risk options that preserve their capital while generating consistent returns. For entrepreneurs aiming to diversify their income, exploring multiple streams can strengthen and expand their financial portfolio.

Lastly, it's beneficial to set clear financial goals when pursuing passive income. Whether your aim is to supplement a hobby expense or replace a full-time income, defining these objectives will guide your strategic decisions. Regularly reviewing progress ensures alignment with your long-term vision.

In conclusion, selecting the right passive income stream requires careful consideration of your interests, skills, resources, risk appetite, and market trends. By thoughtfully aligning these elements, you can embark on a journey towards financial freedom that is both fulfilling and sustainable.

(Chen, 2003)

Strategic Approach to Passive Income Generation

When it comes to building wealth through passive income, maximizing the potential of your chosen income streams requires strategic planning and execution. One effective approach involves diversification. By spreading your investments across multiple income sources, you can reduce your reliance on any single stream and mitigate risk. For instance, real estate investments may promise high returns but are also associated with significant financial capital risks and liquidity challenges (Chen, 2003). Diversifying into digital products, peer-to-peer lending, or dividend stocks can stabilize your earnings. As Marguerita Cheng notes, relying solely on one passive income stream can expose you to vulnerabilities should market conditions shift unfavorably, making a diversified approach key (Cheng, 2025).

Alongside diversification, reinvesting earnings can significantly amplify your gains over time. Compounding returns involve reinvesting profits back into the same income streams, allowing for growth beyond initial expectations. This strategy is particularly potent with dividend-paying stocks or rental income. With dividends, investors can opt to purchase more shares, increasing future dividend payments due to a larger ownership stake. Similarly, applying rental income towards property improvements or acquiring additional properties can enhance value and rental potential. According to Todd Tresidder, even though passive income often requires considerable upfront work, consistent reinvestment optimizes long-term benefits and creates robust cash flow (Royal, 2022).

Staying informed and adaptable is crucial in maximizing passive income opportunities. Maintaining relevance demands continuous learning and market monitoring. Economic conditions, technological advancements, and consumer preferences can fluctuate rapidly, influencing the profitability of various income streams. Engaging with financial literature, attending workshops, or following industry news helps keep strategies aligned with current trends. For example, digital products and online courses may gain traction during times of increased remote working, emphasizing the importance of adapting strategies accordingly. As Chen emphasizes, being positive yet pragmatic allows individuals to build upon their successes while mitigating unforeseen risks (Chen, 2003).

Setting clear financial goals is another essential step in optimizing passive income streams. Without specific objectives, tracking progress and measuring success becomes challenging. Establishing benchmarks such as desired annual returns, savings targets for retirement, or specific investment amounts can guide decision-making and ensure alignment with long-term aspirations. Regularly reviewing these goals enables timely adjustments and enhances accountability. This review process allows individuals to assess whether particular income streams remain viable or require reevaluation. Furthermore, clearly defined goals help in discerning how new trends might fit into your overall strategy, keeping efforts focused on achieving a well-rounded financial portfolio.

While these strategic steps provide a foundational framework, understanding individual circumstances is paramount. Each passive income avenue presents unique advantages and challenges, contingent on personal factors like time availability, skills, and finances. For young professionals striving to transcend paycheck dependency, models requiring lower initial costs or skills-based approaches could be appealing. Creating an app or launching a YouTube channel might align well with their digital proficiency and desire to invest time upfront. Entrepreneurs interested in diversifying their portfolios may lean towards avenues offering potentially higher yields, such as real estate or dividend stocks, balancing them with diligent risk management and assessment of market demand.

Final Insights

This chapter has delved into the varied avenues of passive income, shedding light on key options such as real estate rentals, dividend stocks, peer-to-peer lending, and digital product creation. Each of these income streams offers unique benefits and potential challenges. Real estate stands out with its promise of steady monthly income and property value appreciation, though it requires active management. Dividend stocks provide a stable cash flow combined with opportunities for stock growth, appealing to those less willing to take risks. Peer-to-peer lending presents higher interest returns but comes with the need for careful borrower assessment to manage default risks. Digital products offer creative expression and ongoing sales without the costs associated with physical goods, making it an attractive choice for those looking to share knowledge or talents.

For young professionals aiming to break free from financial constraints, middle-aged individuals planning for retirement, and entrepreneurs expanding their income portfolios, understanding these passive income streams is vital. The chapter highlights the importance of aligning personal interests, skills, initial investment capabilities, and risk tolerance with the right passive income source. It underscores strategic planning, including diversification and reinvestment of earnings, as essential to maximizing potential income and mitigating risks. By thoughtfully considering these elements, readers can make informed decisions, setting them on the path to financial independence and stability.

Reference List

30 Passive Income Ideas to Build Wealth in 2022 . (n.d.). Shopify. https://www.shopify.com/blog/passive-income-ideas

Chen, J. (2003, November 25). *Passive Income* . Investopedia. https://www.investopedia.com/terms/p/passiveincome.asp

Royal, J. (2022, June 23). *14 Passive Income Ideas To Help You Make Money In 2021* . Bankrate. https://www.bankrate.com/investing/passive-income-ideas/

Stanley, J. (2024, September 22). *The Quest for Passive Income Investments: Pros and Cons* . Medium. https://medium.com/@JPStanleyX/the-quest-for-passive-income-investments-pros-and-cons-b5d120345666

Wride, J. (2022, September 21). *Passive Income Strategies: 7 Pros and Cons You Need to Know* . Crafted Finance. https://craftedfinance.com/biggest-pros-and-cons-of-7-different-passive-income-strategies/

Yash, D. (2024, November 12). *Different Ways to Generate Passive Income - Digital Yash - Medium* . Medium. https://medium.com/@yash.mars1825/different-ways-to-generate-passive-income-631c6da5235c

Chapter 4

Real Estate Investment Strategies

Investing in real estate is a powerful strategy for building wealth and achieving financial independence. The world of real estate offers diverse opportunities, each with the potential to significantly impact one's financial portfolio. Yet, it is not without its complexities. Successful real estate investment requires strategic vision, an understanding of market dynamics, and calculated decision-making. Whether you are taking your first steps into this realm or looking to expand your existing investments, knowledge is key. This chapter will guide you through the essential strategies needed to navigate the lucrative landscape of real estate, helping you maximize your investment potential.

In this chapter, you'll explore how to identify promising real estate opportunities that align with your financial goals. We'll delve into the importance of conducting thorough market research, considering factors like location demand, demographic shifts, and infrastructure developments. You'll discover various property types' unique benefits and challenges, from residential to commercial, and learn about networking's critical role in accessing exclusive deals. Additionally, we'll examine the transformative power of technology in today's investment landscape, highlighting tools and platforms that can streamline your analysis and management processes. By the end of this chapter, you'll be equipped with practical insights and strategies to confidently pursue real estate investment as a means to secure and grow your wealth.

Identifying Lucrative Real Estate Opportunities

Embarking on the journey of real estate investment can be both exciting and daunting. Successfully spotting high-potential investments requires a strategic approach combining market knowledge, professional networking, and leveraging technology.

Conducting thorough market research is essential to identify promising opportunities. Start by analyzing location and demand, as these are pivotal in determining property value. Consider demographic shifts—are young professionals moving into an area? If so, this could indicate high rental demand, making multi-family properties attractive (Know Your Market: How to Identify the Perfect Investment Property, 2024). Observe infrastructure developments, zoning changes, or tax incentives, which could signal upcoming property value increases. For instance, if a new transit line is planned, properties nearby might appreciate over time.

Understanding emerging neighborhood trends is also crucial. Neighborhoods with increasing amenities like new cafes, galleries, or parks often experience gentrification, leading to higher property values. Conducting market research to discern these patterns allows investors to capitalize on future hotspots before prices peak (Know Your

Market: How to Identify the Perfect Investment Property, 2024).

Evaluating various property types helps align investments with specific goals. Residential properties, like single-family homes, are typically easier to acquire and manage, appealing to novice investors. They offer steady demand from families and young professionals, making them a reliable entry point. In contrast, commercial properties often promise higher returns but come with greater complexities and risks. These are more suited for seasoned investors looking for robust income streams.

Multi-family units present another attractive option, offering economies of scale and diversified income through multiple tenants. Although requiring more complex management, they can provide substantial returns, especially in areas with high rental demand. Investors should weigh potential earnings against management challenges and decide based on their financial goals and risk tolerance. The tale of the cap rate is a fundamental principle here—it provides insights into the potential return versus associated risks (Know Your Market: How to Identify the Perfect Investment Property, 2024).

Networking with real estate professionals is invaluable in gaining deep insights into market dynamics. Engaging with agents, brokers, and experienced investors can unlock access to exclusive off-market deals and insider information. Attend industry seminars, join real estate investment groups, and build relationships that could lead to lucrative opportunities (The Impact of Technology on Real Estate Investment: Trends and Innovations | Ben Reinberg, 2024).

Utilizing technology is transformative in today's investment landscape. Data visualization tools and online platforms have revolutionized market analysis, offering detailed insights into property and neighborhood trends. Websites like Zillow and Realtor.com enable easy access to current listings and historical sales data, helping investors make informed decisions. Additionally, local Multiple Listing Services (MLS) are valuable resources for understanding market activities.

Embrace digital advancements such as virtual reality tours and digital twins to assess properties remotely, reducing the time spent on initial evaluations. These technologies facilitate comprehensive planning and alterations based on feedback before acquisition decisions, making the market more accessible and strategic (The Impact of Technology on Real Estate Investment: Trends and Innovations | Ben Reinberg, 2024).

Incorporating mobile applications can streamline property management and maintenance tasks. These apps enhance communication with tenants and provide real-time updates on property upkeep, ensuring efficient operation and tenant satisfaction.

Real estate investing is undoubtedly a community-driven endeavor. The benefits of networking and utilizing advanced technologies must be harmonized with continuous learning. The market is ever-evolving, and staying updated with emerging trends, technological innovations, and best practices is crucial for sustained success in this field.

Financing and Mortgage Options

Embarking on a journey into the world of real estate investment requires not only ambition but also a clear understanding of the financial aspects that underpin successful ventures. One of the fundamental elements is mastering mortgage basics, beginning with fixed-rate and adjustable-rate loans. Fixed-rate mortgages offer stability with unchanging interest rates over the life of the loan, making it easier to plan long-term investments. Conversely, adjustable-rate mortgages (ARMs) come with fluctuating interest rates that can lead to lower initial payments. However, they carry higher risk as rates could increase over time, impacting profitability. Choosing between these options depends heavily on market conditions and your personal risk tolerance.

Creative financing solutions provide alternative approaches to traditional funding, especially useful for those looking to make their move with minimal upfront capital. Seller financing involves the seller acting as the lender, allowing the buyer to make direct payments to them. This method can be advantageous when traditional bank financing is challenging to secure. Lease options present another creative avenue by allowing investors to lease a property with an option to purchase it later, often letting part of the rent contribute to the eventual down payment. Joint ventures allow investors to pool resources, spreading both risk and reward among the partners involved. Each of these methods can be tailored to fit specific financial situations, maximizing flexibility and potential returns (Real Estate Investing 101: The Beginner's Guide to Building Wealth, 2024).

Calculating investment costs accurately is imperative for understanding the return on investment (ROI). Initial expenditures include the down payment, closing costs, and any immediate repairs or renovations necessary for the property. Ongoing expenses such as property taxes, insurance, maintenance, and management fees must also be factored in. By subtracting these costs from rental income or future sale profits, investors can gauge their net yield. It's crucial to account for unexpected expenses or vacancies in your calculations to ensure a realistic picture of potential ROI.

A vital aspect of securing favorable loan terms is building a strong credit profile. Creditworthiness directly influences the interest rates lenders will offer, which can significantly impact overall investment costs. Regularly reviewing your credit report, paying bills on time, and minimizing debt levels are effective strategies to improve your credit score. Higher credit scores typically translate to lower interest rates, reducing borrowing costs and increasing potential profits over time. Moreover, maintaining good credit allows more room for negotiation with lenders, providing leverage to obtain better terms aligned with your investment strategy (11 Creative Financing Strategies for Real Estate Investing, n.d.).

When accessing off-market opportunities through established relationships, it's essential to follow a strategic guideline. First, cultivate a network within the real estate industry—this could include agents, brokers, other investors, and property managers. These contacts can provide insights and leads on properties not yet listed publicly. Second, maintain consistent

Personal Finance Strategies

communication and demonstrate credibility in your interactions to build trust and encourage information sharing. Lastly, seize opportunities swiftly once identified, ensuring you conduct thorough due diligence before committing to a deal.

Managing Properties for Steady Income

Understanding the intricacies of property management is essential for anyone seeking consistent income from real estate investments. Managing a property involves several aspects that, when done correctly, ensure not only a steady flow of rental income but also the preservation and appreciation of the property's value over time. At the core, property management revolves around maintaining the property, upholding tenant rights, ensuring timely rent collection, and managing lease renewals.

Maintenance is a fundamental aspect of property management. It entails routine checks and necessary repairs to keep the property in optimal condition, thus preventing small issues from escalating into costly repairs. By prioritizing regular maintenance, property managers can sustain tenant satisfaction, resulting in longer tenancy periods and reduced vacancy rates. Furthermore, understanding tenant rights is crucial to fostering a positive landlord-tenant relationship. This includes respecting tenants' privacy, addressing their concerns promptly, and complying with housing regulations—all of which contribute to a harmonious living environment.

Rent collection is another pivotal element. Establishing a clear and systematic method for collecting rent ensures financial reliability. Implementing technological solutions like online payment portals can streamline this process, making it convenient for both tenants and landlords. Additionally, diligently managing lease renewals allows property managers to maintain stability and continuity within the tenant base, reducing turnover costs and securing long-term income.

Screening tenants effectively is vital in securing reliable occupants who will respect the property and fulfill their financial responsibilities. A thorough screening process includes background checks, credit evaluations, and references from previous landlords. Such measures are indispensable in assessing a prospective tenant's reliability and suitability. Clear communication strategies during the screening phase can set the tone for future interactions, establishing mutual expectations and trust between parties. By adhering to fair housing laws and maintaining consistency in screening criteria, landlords protect themselves from potential discrimination claims while ensuring a fair and unbiased selection process (Michalski, 2023).

Maximizing rental income goes beyond simple rent collection; it requires strategic planning and market awareness. Setting competitive yet reasonable rents attracts quality tenants while optimizing the property's earning potential. Offering diverse lease options, such as short-term rentals or furnished units, can cater to different market segments and increase demand. Moreover, investing in premium amenities like high-speed internet, modern appliances, or pet-friendly spaces can justify higher rent prices, enhancing the property's appeal and profitability (Steadily & Harper, 2024).

Utilizing property management tools and software offers significant advantages in simplifying and streamlining various tasks. These technologies facilitate efficient income tracking, tenant communication, and maintenance request handling. By leveraging these tools, property managers can automate repetitive tasks, reduce the likelihood of errors, and focus more on strategic decision-making. For instance, digital platforms enable property owners to monitor financial performance effortlessly, providing insights into cash flow and profitability trends. Similarly, centralized communication systems ensure swift responses to tenant inquiries or concerns, thereby improving tenant satisfaction and retention rates.

As investors explore real estate opportunities, incorporating analytics-rich platforms can illuminate intricate patterns and trends in the market. Utilizing technology to access comprehensive data helps pinpoint profitable investment areas and predict future market movements. These analytical tools offer crucial insights that otherwise might remain obscured, empowering investors to make informed decisions and manage their properties with precision.

Utilizing Technology in Real Estate Investments

In the rapidly evolving world of real estate investment, technology plays a crucial role in unlocking opportunities and enhancing decision-making. We live in an age where information is power, and accessing accurate, timely data can make all the difference for investors. One way technology assists in this process is through real estate platforms that offer analytics and listings, providing a detailed insight into market trends and potential investments.

These platforms serve as a gateway to vast amounts of information about property values, neighborhood dynamics, and real estate developments. They empower both young professionals looking to manage their money wisely and middle-aged individuals planning for retirement by offering tools that were once reserved for industry insiders. For entrepreneurs seeking to diversify their income streams, these platforms are invaluable, allowing them to explore options across diverse markets with ease and confidence.

Social media and online forums have also emerged as powerful resources for real-time information on market trends and public sentiment. Investors can join groups or follow pages dedicated to specific areas of interest, such as particular neighborhoods or types of properties. Through these channels, they can gain insights from others' experiences and stay informed about emerging opportunities before they become common knowledge. This kind of engagement is particularly beneficial for those who want to stay ahead of the curve and capitalize on new trends before the general market catches on.

Data visualization tools are another technological advancement that enhances the real estate investment process. These tools take complex datasets and present them in an accessible, visual format, making it easier for investors to identify patterns and trends. By using charts, graphs, and maps, investors can better understand which properties hold value and which areas may offer the most promising returns. This capability is essential for individuals and businesses alike, ensuring that decisions are based on evidence rather than speculation.

The integration of these technologies supports more strategic decision-making, especially for those investing significant sums with the hope of securing their financial future. Entrepreneurs can leverage these tools to assess various investment opportunities systematically, ensuring they allocate their resources where they're likely to see the greatest return.

Innovative applications are also simplifying property management, which is a critical aspect of maintaining consistent income from real estate investments. Apps designed to assist with tasks like tenant communication, maintenance requests, and rent collection help streamline operations, reducing the burden on property owners. These applications are particularly valuable in managing multiple properties, where efficiency and accuracy are essential. By automating routine processes, investors can focus on expanding their portfolios and optimizing their investments.

One of the most compelling aspects of this wave of innovation is its accessibility. The democratization of data means that anyone with internet access can utilize these tools, regardless of their experience level. This opens the door for young professionals eager to escape the paycheck-to-paycheck cycle, giving them the means to make informed investment choices that build wealth over time. For middle-aged individuals, these advancements offer peace of mind, knowing that their savings and investments are being managed meticulously and thoughtfully.

For budding entrepreneurs, the ability to manage diverse investments efficiently means they can pursue ambitious strategies without compromising their primary business ventures. The insights gained through technological tools can help them identify untapped markets, adjust their approaches based on current data, and remain competitive amidst a rapidly changing economic landscape.

These advancements in technology not only enhance individual investment strategies but also influence broader market behaviors. As more investors rely on data-driven approaches, the real estate market itself becomes more dynamic and responsive. Market trends evolve quickly, creating both challenges and opportunities for those involved. By leveraging technology, investors equip themselves to adapt swiftly to these changes, maintaining an edge in a competitive environment.

As we look to the future, it's clear that the intersection of technology and real estate will continue to develop, presenting new possibilities for investors. Embracing these tools today means being better prepared for tomorrow's challenges, ready to seize opportunities as they arise.

Bringing It All Together

Investing in real estate is a pathway to building wealth, and this chapter has provided insights into successfully navigating the field. Understanding the intricacies of spotting lucrative opportunities begins with conducting thorough market research and staying informed about demographic shifts, neighborhood trends, and emerging infrastructure developments. By evaluating various property types, such as residential, commercial, or multi-family units, investors can align their strategies with specific financial goals and risk tolerances.

Networking with professionals offers valuable insider information, while technology provides tools for comprehensive market analysis and efficient property management.

The integration of these elements—market knowledge, strategic networking, and technological advancements—empowers both novice and seasoned investors. Young professionals looking to establish financial stability, middle-aged individuals planning for retirement, and entrepreneurs seeking diversified income streams can all harness these strategies. The key lies in ongoing education, a clear understanding of financial dynamics, and the ability to adapt to changing market conditions. By embracing these practices, investors position themselves for sustained success in real estate, securing their financial future across different stages of life.

Reference List

11 Creative Financing Strategies For Real Estate Investing . (n.d.). Www.landlordstudio.com. https://www.landlordstudio.com/blog/creative-financing-real-estate

Know Your Market: How to Identify the Perfect Investment Property . (2024, April 27). Kiavi.com. https://www.kiavi.com/blog/know-your-market-how-to-identify-the-perfect-investment-property

Michalski, W. (2023, December 27). *Pioneer Real Estate Services* . PioneerBeck. https://

pioneeraustin.com/the-benefits-of-having-a-property-manager-handle-tenant-screening-and-background-checks/

Real Estate Investing 101: The Beginner's Guide to Building Wealth . (2024). Empora Title. https://www.emporatitle.com/blog/real-estate-investing-101-guide-building-wealth

Real estate data visualization | JLL . (n.d.). Www.us.jll.com. https://www.us.jll.com/en/transform-with-technology/visualize

Steadily, & Harper, Z. (2024, October 31). *The Benefits of Hiring a Property Manager for Your Rental* . Steadily.com. https://www.steadily.com/blog/the-benefits-of-hiring-a-property-manager-for-your-rental

The Impact of Technology on Real Estate Investment: Trends and Innovations | Ben Reinberg . (2024). Benreinberg.com. https://www.benreinberg.com/blogs/the-impact-of-technology-on-real-estate-investment-trends-and-innovations

bt3xblogposter. (2024, November 29). *How Data Analytics is Shaping the Future of Real Estate* . Real Estate Investing for Women. https://realestateinvestingwomen.com/how-data-analytics-is-shaping-the-future-of-real-estate/

Chapter 5

Navigating the Stock Market

Navigating the stock market is an endeavor that can shape one's financial journey, offering both opportunities and challenges. The market acts as a bustling arena where stocks are actively traded, providing a platform for investors to engage with the corporate world and unlock growth potential. With its myriad components and complex dynamics, understanding the stock market is crucial for anyone looking to make informed investment decisions. It isn't just about buying or selling; it's about comprehending how this intricate system functions, knowing when to enter or exit positions, and grasping how different factors can influence stock prices. For many, the allure of investing in the stock market lies in the prospect of building wealth and securing financial freedom over time. Yet, this pursuit requires more than mere enthusiasm – it demands strategic insight and knowledge.

In this chapter, readers will delve into strategies essential for successful stock market investments. The discussion unfolds by explaining the nature of stocks and the role they play in an investor's portfolio, emphasizing the need to distinguish between common and preferred stocks. Readers will gain insights on opening brokerage accounts and selecting platforms that align with their trading preferences. Additionally, mastering key stock market terminology is highlighted as fundamental, allowing investors to understand concepts like dividends and capital gains thoroughly. Trading styles and approaches—ranging from short-term speculative trades to long-term wealth-building strategies—are explored, enabling readers to identify which fits best with their goals. By offering a comprehensive overview of these topics, readers will emerge equipped with actionable knowledge to better navigate the complexities of stock market investing, tailored to their individual risk tolerances and financial aspirations.

Basics of Stock Investing

Navigating the stock market can seem daunting, especially for those new to investing. However, understanding how stock markets operate is essential to building a solid investment strategy. The stock market functions as a platform where shares of public companies are bought and sold, providing opportunities for investors to gain part ownership in these companies. This exchange is facilitated by stock exchanges like the New York Stock Exchange (NYSE) and Nasdaq, which serve as arenas for trading shares between investors in the secondary market. Such markets play a crucial role in modern capitalism by enabling companies to raise capital and allowing individuals to participate in corporate growth.

To fully leverage the stock market, it's vital to understand the key differences between common and preferred stocks. Common stocks represent ownership in a company and usually come with voting rights at shareholder meetings. While they offer the potential for dividends and capital gains, they also carry a higher risk due to market

Personal Finance Strategies

volatility. On the other hand, preferred stocks typically do not provide voting rights but offer a fixed dividend, which can be more reliable. Preferred shareholders have a higher claim on assets than common shareholders in the event of liquidation. By differentiating between these stock types, investors can make informed decisions that align with their financial goals and risk tolerance.

Opening a brokerage account is an important step in streamlining the process of buying and selling stocks. Brokerage accounts function as digital platforms that give investors access to stock exchanges and a wide array of financial instruments. Selecting the right brokerage involves evaluating factors such as fees, available resources for research, and ease of use. Many brokerages now offer app-based platforms that allow investors to track their portfolios and execute trades on the go. This accessibility empowers investors to react swiftly to market changes, making strategic adjustments as necessary.

Familiarizing oneself with stock market terminology is another foundational aspect of investing. Key terms include dividends, which are company earnings distributed to shareholders; capital gains, the profit from selling a stock at a higher price than its purchase cost; and the price-to-earnings ratio (P/E ratio), a measure used to determine if a stock is overvalued or undervalued compared to others. Understanding these concepts is crucial for analyzing a company's performance and potential growth, assisting investors in making well-informed decisions.

Furthermore, appreciating how stocks are traded can enhance one's investment acumen. Trading typically falls into two categories: short-term trading and long-term investing. Short-term traders, or day traders, buy and sell stocks within short periods, often focusing on technical analysis to predict price movements. Meanwhile, long-term investors focus on buying stocks to hold for several years, banking on consistent growth and reinvestment of dividends to build wealth over time. Recognizing the distinctions between these approaches, investors can tailor their strategies to match their objectives and time horizons.

Building a Diversified Portfolio

In the dynamic world of stock market investments, diversification stands out as a crucial strategy for managing risk and enhancing potential returns. Diversification means spreading investments across various asset classes to minimize the impact that any single underperforming asset can have on your overall portfolio. This approach not only helps in cushioning against market fluctuations but also opens up avenues for growth by tapping into different sectors and regions.

The strength of diversification lies in its ability to create a safety net. When one asset class, such as stocks, faces a downturn, others like bonds or mutual funds might remain stable or even gain value. A well-diversified portfolio can potentially offset losses from certain investments with gains from others, ensuring a smoother financial journey. As an example, during an economic slowdown, bond prices often rise because they are perceived as safer investments compared to stocks, which may decline. By holding both, an investor can reduce volatility in their portfolio.

Personal Finance Strategies

When constructing a diversified portfolio, it is vital to consider various asset classes. Stocks, bonds, mutual funds, and exchange-traded funds (ETFs) each offer unique benefits and risks. Stocks represent ownership in a company and provide dividends and capital appreciation opportunities. Bonds, loans made to government entities or corporations, usually offer fixed interest payments, adding stability. Mutual funds pool money from multiple investors to purchase a variety of securities, providing instant diversification. ETFs are similar to mutual funds but trade on exchanges like stocks, offering flexibility and diverse exposure without significant investment amounts. Each of these asset classes contributes differently to a portfolio's performance, thus balancing risk and potential returns.

An integral part of diversification is aligning your portfolio with your individual risk tolerance and financial goals. Risk tolerance varies; some investors prefer aggressive strategies with higher risks, while others seek more conservative approaches focusing on preserving capital. For instance, young professionals, eager to maximize long-term growth, might lean toward a higher stock allocation due to their longer investment horizon. In contrast, individuals nearing retirement might focus on conserving wealth through bonds and other low-risk assets. By clearly defining your financial objectives—be it saving for retirement, buying a home, or financing education—you can tailor a portfolio mix that suits your comfort and ensures you stay on track toward achieving your dreams.

Regular portfolio reviews and adjustments are essential to maintaining a diversified strategy. The financial markets are ever-changing, influenced by economic shifts, geopolitical events, and industry developments. Regular assessments help investors stay informed about how these changes affect their portfolios. Holding periodic sessions—quarterly or biannually—is a pragmatic approach, allowing investors to rebalance their portfolios if necessary. Rebalancing involves realigning the portfolio to its original target allocation by selling high-performing assets and buying underperforming ones. This practice prevents any single asset class from dominating the portfolio, preserving its intended risk level.

For instance, suppose an initial portfolio allocation was 60% stocks and 40% bonds. If over time, stock values soar, the portfolio might shift to 70% stocks and 30% bonds. In this scenario, rebalancing would involve selling some stocks and purchasing additional bonds to restore the 60/40 balance. This disciplined approach not only manages risks but also capitalizes on market opportunities, optimizing the portfolio's performance over time.

Risk Management in Stock Trading

Navigating the stock market can be a daunting task, but equipping yourself with solid strategies to protect your investments is crucial. Understanding the risks associated with stock trading helps prepare for market volatility, ensuring you're better positioned against sudden downturns. Market volatility refers to the rapid and significant price movements in the stock market, which can either benefit or harm your investments. Factors such as economic changes, political events, or corporate developments influence this volatility. Recognizing these various risks, including market risk, credit risk, and liquidity risk, is the first step toward safeguarding your portfolio. By being aware of these potential pitfalls, you position yourself to respond proactively rather than reactively.

One effective technique traders use to manage these risks is implementing stop-loss orders. A stop-loss order is an automated function that sells a stock once it reaches a specified price, thus limiting potential losses on an investment. This tool not only helps automate loss management but also encourages disciplined trading by setting predetermined exit points based on careful analysis rather than emotional response. Many successful traders attribute their ability to maintain discipline in part to using strategic stop-loss orders. For example, if you purchase a stock at $50 and set a stop-loss order at $45, should the stock price drop to $45, your shares will automatically sell, capping your loss at $5 per share. This proactive measure ensures that you limit your downside risk without constantly monitoring the market.

Moreover, determining the appropriate size of your individual investments relative to your overall portfolio—known as position sizing—is vital for effective risk management. Position sizing involves carefully calculating the proportion of your total capital allocated to each trade, balancing potential returns with acceptable levels of risk. One common strategy employed by day traders is the one-percent rule, which suggests that no more than 1% of your capital should be used in a single trade (Kuepper, 2019). This means if your trading account holds $10,000, you shouldn't risk more than $100 on any given position. Such an approach helps mitigate the impact of any single loss, protecting the integrity of your broader investment strategy. Additionally, understanding gap risk—where stock prices jump unexpectedly between trading sessions—further refines your approach to maintaining a stable portfolio (Chen, 2019).

In addition to utilizing stop-loss orders and practicing prudent position sizing, thorough market research and analysis play crucial roles in making informed decisions. The ability to conduct comprehensive research allows investors to identify both opportunities and risks within the market landscape. Effective market analysis includes evaluating financial statements, understanding industry trends, and keeping abreast of global economic indicators. This foundational understanding empowers investors to make educated choices rather than relying solely on intuition or hearsay. Furthermore, employing analytical tools, such as technical indicators or chart patterns, provides visual representation to aid decision-making processes. These resources allow traders to discern patterns or trends that may not be readily apparent through cursory examination alone.

For those serious about developing a robust investment strategy, choosing the right broker is essential. Brokers serve as the intermediary between you and the stock market, so it's critical to select one that aligns with your trading style and frequency. Some brokers are better suited for frequent trading, offering competitive commissions and cutting-edge analytical tools tailored for active traders. Conversely, others cater to investors who trade less often, providing resources focused on long-term investing. Therefore, scrutinizing aspects like commission rates, technology platforms, customer service, and educational resources aids in making an informed choice about which brokerage fits your specific needs.

While the aforementioned techniques address immediate and tactical considerations for protecting investments, maintaining a broader perspective is equally important. Diversification remains a key strategic element, ensuring that your portfolio isn't overly dependent on any single asset or sector. By diversifying across different industries, market capitalizations, and geographic regions, you reduce exposure to localized risks that might disproportionately affect a concentrated portfolio. However, even diversified portfolios require regular review and adjustment to remain aligned with evolving market conditions and personal financial goals.

Market Research and Analysis

Investment in the stock market requires a strategic approach, combining thorough research and robust analysis to make informed decisions. This subpoint delves into the critical aspects of enhancing investment decision-making by equipping investors with essential tools and knowledge for navigating the financial landscape.

First and foremost, embracing comprehensive research is pivotal to identifying potential risks and rewards associated with stock market investments. A common pitfall for novice investors is overlooking due diligence, which can lead to unforeseen losses. By methodically researching different stocks, industries, and market trends, investors can gain valuable insights that inform their strategies. For instance, understanding a company's financial statements, management team, competitive position, and market conditions enables investors to anticipate performance outcomes more accurately. As emphasized in "The Comprehensive Guide to Investment Research" (n.d.), investment research serves as the bedrock for sound financial analysis, empowering investors to allocate capital effectively, maximize returns, and mitigate risks.

Furthermore, the utilization of analytical tools plays a significant role in refining investment decision-making processes. Tools such as fundamental analysis and technical analysis provide frameworks for evaluating stocks. Fundamental analysis involves assessing a company's intrinsic value based on economic indicators, financial health, and market position, while technical analysis focuses on statistical trends gathered from trading activity, such as price movement and volume. These tools aid investors in interpreting data, predicting future price movements, and determining appropriate entry and exit points for stocks. Machine learning and artificial intelligence have further advanced these capabilities by enabling swift processing and interpretation of vast datasets, thus enhancing decision accuracy (*The Comprehensive Guide to Investment Research*, n.d.).

Staying informed with current market news is equally crucial in anticipating risks and seizing opportunities. The financial world is dynamic, with market conditions changing rapidly due to economic, political, and technological shifts. Regularly following business news, industry reports, and expert analyses can provide investors with timely information that influences stock prices. For example, announcements about mergers and acquisitions, regulatory changes, or new product launches can significantly impact a company's stock value. Engaging with trusted financial news sources ensures that investors remain aware of such developments and adjust their strategies accordingly.

Moreover, keeping abreast of updates on economic indicators and corporate performances is vital for proactive decision-making. Economic indicators such as GDP growth rates, interest rates, inflation, and employment figures offer insights into the broader economic environment influencing stock markets. Similarly, tracking corporate earnings reports, balance sheets, and cash flow statements reveals a company's performance trajectory over time. Analyzing these metrics helps investors predict potential stock movements and make adjustments to their portfolios to align with their risk appetite and investment goals.

Incorporating these practices not only strengthens investment strategies but also fosters confidence among investors, particularly those seeking financial security and independence. Young professionals, middle-aged individuals planning for retirement, and entrepreneurs exploring additional income streams all benefit from a disciplined approach to stock market investments. By prioritizing research, leveraging analytical tools, staying informed with market news, and regularly updating economic and corporate data, investors can optimize their portfolios and navigate the complexities of the stock market with greater assurance.

Summary and Reflections

In this chapter, we have explored various strategies for navigating the complex landscape of stock market investments. Understanding the fundamentals such as the differences between common and preferred stocks, the role of brokerage accounts, and essential market terminology lays the groundwork for informed investing. We've discussed how diversifying your portfolio across different asset classes can manage risk effectively, ensuring a balanced approach towards potential returns. These foundational strategies are crucial for anyone looking to build wealth through the stock market, whether you're a young professional seeking financial independence, a middle-aged individual planning for retirement, or an entrepreneur aiming to expand your income streams.

Moreover, we've delved into the importance of risk management by highlighting techniques like using stop-loss orders and maintaining an appropriate position size in your investments. These tactics help protect your portfolio from unexpected market volatility. The necessity of thorough market research and analysis has been emphasized to empower investors with the knowledge needed to make sound decisions. By staying informed on economic indicators and corporate performances, investors can adapt their strategies to changing market conditions. As you continue your investment journey, applying these strategies will be vital in achieving your financial goals with confidence and resilience.

Reference List

Chen, J. (2020, October 6). *Equity Market Definition*. Investopedia. https://www.investopedia.com/terms/e/equitymarket.asp

Chen, J. (2019). *What is Investment Position Sizing?* Investopedia. https://www.investopedia.com/terms/p/positionsizing.asp

Diversification Strategies for Your Investment Portfolio | U.S. Bank. (2024, August 19). Usbank.com. https://www.usbank.com/investing/financial-perspectives/investing-insights/diversification-strategy.html

Kuepper, J. (2019). *Risk management techniques for active traders*. Investopedia. https://www.investopedia.com/articles/trading/09/risk-management.asp

Stock Market 101: Understanding The Fundamentals Of Equities Trading - DLM - A Development Investment Bank. (2023, November 2). DLM - a Development Investment Bank. https://dlm.group/stock-market-101/

Segal, T. (2023, July 1). *What Is Diversification? Definition as Investing Strategy*. Investopedia. https://www.investopedia.com/terms/d/diversification.asp

The Comprehensive Guide to Investment Research . (n.d.). Corporate Finance Institute. https://corporatefinanceinstitute.com/resources/capital_markets/comprehensive-guide-to-investment-research/

Twin, A. (2019). *Investment Analysis: The Key to Sound Portfolio Management Strategy* . Investopedia. https://www.investopedia.com/terms/i/investment-analysis.asp

Chapter 6

Embracing Entrepreneurship for Income Diversification

Embracing entrepreneurship is a path abundant with potential for diversifying income. In today's dynamic economic landscape, individuals of all ages are exploring entrepreneurial ventures as a means to enhance their financial security. This chapter delves into the art of identifying business opportunities, an essential skill for those seeking to break away from traditional income streams. Whether it's young professionals desiring freedom from living paycheck-to-paycheck, middle-aged individuals planning for retirement, or seasoned entrepreneurs looking to expand their portfolios, understanding how to spot and harness potential opportunities is key to success.

This chapter focuses on several important aspects critical to expanding one's income through entrepreneurship. Readers will discover the significance of market research techniques in evaluating high-potential ideas, enabling them to discern lucrative opportunities and tailor their solutions to meet consumer demands. Attention will also be paid to identifying market gaps where current products or services fall short, encouraging innovation and improved offerings. The discussion extends to the influence of demographics in guiding product development, ensuring that endeavors align with consumer needs. Finally, by examining emerging trends and leveraging personal skills and passions, aspiring entrepreneurs can sharpen their vision and position themselves advantageously within evolving markets. Engaging with networks and embracing technological advancements further enrich this exploration, offering insights that could lead to transformative business ventures.

Identifying Business Opportunities

To identify and evaluate high-potential business ideas, understanding market research techniques is fundamental. For young professionals seeking to break free from the paycheck-to-paycheck lifestyle, and for middle-aged individuals planning their retirement, discerning lucrative opportunities can be transformative. Entrepreneurs aiming to diversify income streams find that knowing their target audience's preferences and unmet needs sharpens their entrepreneurial vision.

Begin with comprehensive market research. This involves gathering data on consumer preferences and behaviors, which unveils trends and patterns crucial for developing innovative business ideas. Techniques like surveys, focus groups, and competitor analysis help determine what consumers value and where their demands lie. By understanding these dynamics, you can identify profitable niches that align with your skills and interests, setting a solid foundation for any business venture.

Identifying gaps in the market is another critical component of this journey. Look around and notice where current products or services fall short or fail to meet customer expectations. This doesn't just mean creating something new but improving existing offerings to better fulfill consumer desires. For instance, if there's a growing demand for sustainable products and yet a dearth in affordable options, addressing this gap could lead to a successful sustainable goods business. It's about marrying insight with innovation to create targeted solutions.

Understanding demographics further supports focused product development. Demographics—age, gender, income level, education—provide insights into who your potential customers are. These segments can guide you in tailoring products or services that directly meet varied needs. Whether targeting millennials looking for tech-savvy solutions or retirees interested in health-focused products, pinpointing demographic details helps fine-tune marketing strategies and product design to resonate with specific groups.

Staying ahead of trends offers a strategic advantage, enabling entrepreneurs to respond proactively to changing market dynamics. Keeping an eye on emerging trends in technology, culture, and economy helps in predicting shifts that could affect consumer behavior. An entrepreneur who anticipates these changes can position their business to take advantage of evolving markets, thus maintaining relevance and competitiveness. Regularly updating your knowledge through industry reports, trade journals, and expert commentary ensures you remain informed and agile.

Another technique to consider is evaluating ideas against your personal skills and passions. A business idea might sound promising on paper, but aligning it with your capabilities and interests increases the likelihood of success and satisfaction.

Evaluate how a proposed business fits within your long-term goals, whether it leverages existing expertise, and if it ignites genuine enthusiasm. This alignment often results in greater commitment and resilience through challenges.

Networking plays a key role in uncovering opportunities. Engaging with other professionals, attending industry events, and joining entrepreneurial groups can provide valuable insights into successful business models and practices. Through networking, entrepreneurs gain access to advice, mentorship, and even collaborations that can accelerate business development and expansion.

Simultaneously, embracing technological advancements can be a game-changer. Technology not only aids in making processes more efficient but also opens doors to online marketplaces and digital marketing tools. This is especially pertinent for young professionals and entrepreneurs who are more adept at leveraging digital platforms to reach wider audiences.

Finally, a systematic evaluation approach such as SWOT analysis (Strengths, Weaknesses, Opportunities, Threats) can offer a structured view of potential business ideas. Assessing internal strengths and weaknesses alongside external opportunities and threats equips entrepreneurs with a comprehensive understanding of the viability and risks associated with their ideas.

Balancing Entrepreneurship with Existing Income

Balancing entrepreneurship with existing income streams requires careful time management, a vital skill that ensures productivity and efficiency.

Personal Finance Strategies

One effective strategy is time-blocking, where you allocate specific chunks of time to different tasks or projects. This approach not only helps in organizing your day but also ensures that each task receives the attention it requires without getting overshadowed by other commitments. Young professionals, eager to break free from the paycheck-to-paycheck cycle, can particularly benefit from time-blocking, as it allows them to juggle both their job responsibilities and entrepreneurial pursuits seamlessly.

For example, if you work a regular nine-to-five job but are passionate about starting a business in the evenings, time-blocking allows you to dedicate specific hours in the evening solely for your new venture. It may involve setting aside two hours each night to focus purely on business development without distractions. By doing so, you create a structured routine that maximizes productivity and minimizes stress. It's especially useful for individuals planning retirement or middle-aged professionals who want to secure financial futures while gradually transitioning into entrepreneurship.

In addition to managing your time effectively, leveraging passive income streams can significantly ease the financial strain during the initial phases of entrepreneurship. Passive income refers to money earned with minimal active involvement, such as through investments like stocks, bonds, or real estate. For instance, an entrepreneur might invest in dividend-paying stocks which provide regular income, thereby offering a financial cushion when cash flow from a new business is still uncertain. This is crucial for people looking to diversify income sources without jeopardizing their primary earnings.

Investments in mutual funds or rental properties are popular avenues for generating passive income. They require initial capital but demand less day-to-day management compared to actively running a business. By having these income streams, entrepreneurs can fund their ventures without depleting savings or taking on excessive debt, ensuring they have a safety net during challenging times. This strategy resonates well with aspiring entrepreneurs who want to build a stable foundation before diving completely into new business ventures.

Understanding how to set realistic expectations around time commitments is another key factor in successful entrepreneurship. It's tempting to throw yourself entirely into a new project, but this approach often leads to burnout and inefficiency. Instead, it's important to gauge how much time you can truly dedicate to your entrepreneurial activities while still fulfilling other responsibilities. Realism in time allocation prevents over-commitment and ensures sustainable progress across all fronts.

Young professionals should start small, perhaps dedicating weekends or specific days to entrepreneurship initially, allowing them to scale gradually based on what they learn about their capacity and needs. Similarly, middle-aged individuals or those nearing retirement might use this transition as an opportunity to test the waters without overwhelming themselves. By acknowledging limitations and working within them, entrepreneurs maintain harmony between their current income streams and new ventures.

Creating a support system is equally essential for those navigating the entrepreneurial landscape. Surrounding oneself with mentors and peers provides invaluable guidance and fosters a growth-oriented mindset. Mentors bring experience and perspective, helping young professionals avoid common pitfalls and make informed decisions. They can offer advice on everything from financial management to strategic planning, acting as a sounding board for ideas and challenges.

Peer networks also play a critical role by providing moral support and practical insights from individuals facing similar journeys. Engaging in entrepreneur-focused communities or local business groups enables networking opportunities that can lead to collaboration, resource sharing, and even partnership possibilities. For someone new to entrepreneurship, these connections are instrumental in building confidence and expanding horizons beyond immediate circles.

Beyond emotional support, mentors and peer groups offer critical feedback on business plans, marketing strategies, and product development. Their diverse backgrounds and experiences enrich your understanding, broadening perspectives and encouraging innovation. For instance, a retired professional entering entrepreneurship could benefit greatly from insights shared offhandedly at a group meeting, sparking new ideas that refine their business model.

Building a Brand and Online Presence

Establishing a strong brand identity and online presence is fundamental for business growth and recognition in today's digital landscape. For young professionals aiming to escape the cycle of living paycheck-to-paycheck, middle-aged individuals planning for retirement, and entrepreneurs eager to create multiple income streams, understanding these concepts is crucial.

Defining your brand through a compelling story can significantly enhance its appeal to your target audience. A well-crafted narrative not only humanizes your brand but also fosters a deeper connection with consumers. Take, for instance, how some iconic brands have leveraged their founders' personal journeys or mission statements to cultivate trust and loyalty. By clearly articulating what your brand stands for, you open avenues for emotional engagement, which often leads to stronger customer relationships.

To effectively define your brand, consider guidelines such as identifying core values that resonate with your audience, creating a distinctive voice that reflects your business's personality, and ensuring consistency across all branding materials. These steps help in crafting a unique identity that is transparent and relatable, thereby instilling confidence in potential customers.

Once your brand identity is clear, utilizing social media platforms becomes an invaluable strategy. These platforms offer low-cost marketing opportunities that can transform followers into loyal customers. Social media allows for direct interaction with your audience, providing real-time feedback and insights into consumer preferences. Successful brands use these channels not just for promotion, but also to build community and engage authentically with users.

When venturing into social media utilization, it's important to follow certain guidelines: choose platforms that align best with your brand's target audience, maintain consistent and engaging content, and interact thoughtfully with your followers. Doing so not only maximizes visibility but also helps foster meaningful connections that can convert casual scrollers into dedicated patrons.

Creating a professional website is another critical component for enhancing accessibility, engagement, and visibility. A well-designed website acts as a virtual storefront, offering potential customers information about products, services, and your brand's mission. User-friendly design and strategic SEO optimization ensure that your website appears prominently in search results, making it easier for new customers to discover your business.

The guidelines for developing a successful website include focusing on intuitive navigation, providing clear and comprehensive content, and optimizing for mobile devices to ensure a seamless experience. SEO strategies like using relevant keywords and obtaining backlinks further help improve your site's ranking, drawing in more organic traffic and boosting overall brand awareness.

In addition to your branding and digital presence, leveraging online marketing tools enhances reach and credibility. Tools such as email campaigns allow for personalized communication with your audience, delivering tailored content and exclusive offers directly to their inboxes. Meanwhile, influencer collaborations provide access to new networks of potential customers, lending authenticity and expanding your brand's influence.

To effectively leverage these tools, adhere to principles like segmenting your email list to meet diverse interests, crafting compelling subject lines to increase open rates, and partnering with influencers whose audiences align with your brand values. When done correctly, these efforts can significantly amplify your marketing reach, strengthening your brand's position in a competitive market.

Evaluating and Developing Business Ideas

Understanding how to assess and develop viable business concepts is a cornerstone for entrepreneurs looking to expand their income through new ventures. To begin with, employing a SWOT analysis can be an invaluable tool in this process. A SWOT analysis allows individuals to dive deep into the strengths, weaknesses, opportunities, and threats related to their business idea. For instance, uncovering strengths may involve recognizing unique skills or resources you possess, such as expertise in a niche market or access to advanced technology. This recognition helps you leverage these advantages effectively.

Conversely, identifying weaknesses could highlight areas that require improvement or additional support, like gaps in knowledge or limited initial funding. By acknowledging these aspects early on, entrepreneurs can seek training or partnerships to mitigate potential drawbacks. Opportunities, often external factors like emerging markets or technological advancements, offer pathways to growth and innovation if seized at the right moment. Meanwhile, understanding threats—be it competition, regulatory changes, or economic shifts—enables more strategic planning and risk management.

Awareness of potential risks is another essential component in nurturing a sustainable business model. Entrepreneurs must prepare themselves for various challenges they might encounter. Recognizing these risks involves evaluating both internal and external factors that could impact the business. Consider the example of a start-up depending heavily on a single supplier; disruption in supply chains could jeopardize operations. Anticipating such scenarios allows entrepreneurs to establish contingencies, like developing multiple supplier relationships or maintaining an emergency inventory.

Conducting viability studies goes hand-in-hand with risk assessment. These studies are crucial for guiding resource allocation, ensuring both time and capital are used efficiently. Viability studies typically include market research, financial projections, and feasibility assessments. These elements provide a comprehensive overview of whether a business idea is likely to succeed. For those assessing a concept, conducting detailed customer surveys or pilot programs can offer insights into consumer needs and preferences, confirming demand for the product or service before significant investments are made.

Financial projections within viability studies also allow budding entrepreneurs to forecast cash flows and budget requirements accurately. Such analyses help identify break-even points, ensuring that the venture remains financially viable in the long term. Understanding these metrics empowers entrepreneurs to allocate resources judiciously, avoiding overextension while maximizing profitability. Furthermore, a well-structured viability study serves as a compelling argument when seeking investment from stakeholders or financial institutions.

Networking is yet another pivotal strategy for developing viable business concepts. Networking not only expands one's circle but also creates opportunities for collaboration and partnership, which can enhance brand visibility immensely. Engaging with industry peers, mentors, and potential partners can lead to valuable exchanges of ideas and shared resources. For example, attending industry conferences or joining entrepreneur groups can open doors to collaborations that might bring about innovative solutions and co-branding opportunities.

These connections often facilitate knowledge exchange and firsthand insight into industry trends, enabling entrepreneurs to stay informed about new developments and practices. Networking can also be instrumental in securing endorsements, testimonials, or even introductions to prospective clients. Additionally, building a solid network supports the formation of alliances that can increase business credibility and trust within the marketplace.

Bringing It All Together

Throughout this chapter, we have explored various ways to expand income through entrepreneurial ventures, offering insights into how individuals can identify and capitalize on business opportunities. Whether you're a young professional aiming to break free from living paycheck-to-paycheck, a middle-aged individual planning for retirement, or an entrepreneur seeking to diversify your income streams, understanding the importance of market research, demographics, and technological advancements is crucial. These elements help you pinpoint profitable niches and refine your business strategies. By leveraging both personal skills and networking opportunities, one can uncover promising ideas that align with their passions, setting the stage for successful business development.

In pursuing entrepreneurial success, balancing existing commitments with new ventures is key. Effective time management, such as time-blocking, helps allocate focus between regular responsibilities and entrepreneurial goals, ensuring a manageable transition. Diversifying income through passive sources, like investments, provides financial stability, supporting business efforts without risking primary earnings. Setting realistic expectations around time commitments prevents burnout and promotes steady progress, while creating a supportive network of mentors and peers bolsters confidence and innovation. With these strategies in mind, entrepreneurs are well-equipped to embark on ventures that enhance their financial future, all while maintaining harmony between current duties and new aspirations.

Chapter 7

Retirement Planning and Early Financial Independence

Retirement planning and early financial independence are pivotal goals for many individuals striving to secure a prosperous future. This chapter addresses the importance of setting these financial objectives and lays the groundwork for achieving them. For young professionals, breaking free from the paycheck-to-paycheck cycle often requires adopting a mindset focused on long-term security rather than immediate gratification. It involves understanding the nuances of financial freedom and grasping how early planning can unlock opportunities that extend beyond conventional career paths. Meanwhile, middle-aged individuals grapple with the reality of ensuring their savings will not just suffice but flourish, supporting a lifestyle they have envisioned throughout their working years.

Within this framework, readers will explore actionable strategies for defining clear retirement goals aligned with personal aspirations. The chapter delves into techniques such as visualizing one's ideal retirement scenario, which serves as a powerful motivator in setting achievable savings targets. Moreover, it highlights the significance of establishing a target retirement age, an element that shapes financial decisions significantly across one's career span. By examining potential adjustments in projected benefits like Social Security, this chapter offers insights into maintaining flexibility amid unforeseen life events, thus reinforcing how adaptability is crucial in financial planning. Additionally, by estimating healthcare and living expenses, readers gain a comprehensive perspective on structuring a robust financial plan, securing peace of mind in retirement.

Setting Retirement Goals

When planning for retirement, it's essential to establish clear and achievable goals that align closely with your individual financial aspirations. Visualization of your ideal retirement can serve as a powerful tool in setting realistic savings targets. Picture where you would like to live, the activities you wish to pursue, or even the causes you want to support. This visualization not only inspires but also provides a practical framework to determine how much money you'll need to accumulate. For instance, if you envision traveling annually, owning a home in a serene location, or continuing education, these elements will directly impact your financial calculations. Organizing your goals around this vision can transform abstract desires into actionable plans, allowing for more precise budget and savings estimations.

Setting a target retirement age is another cornerstone of effective planning. Knowing when you aim to retire can significantly influence your saving patterns and financial decisions throughout your career. Deciding on a retirement age often reflects a balance between financial readiness and personal desires. For many, the goal might be to retire early, while others may find fulfillment in extending their careers longer. Understanding the implications of retiring at different ages, such as potential adjustments to projected Social Security benefits, helps mold a disciplined savings habit. Early decision-making in this area can provide clarity and motivation, ensuring that each saving or investment choice aligns with future plans. It could mean choosing to contribute more towards retirement accounts or cutting down on current expenses to reach those long-term objectives.

Another critical factor in establishing retirement goals is estimating healthcare and living expenses. These costs are substantial in shaping how much wealth one needs to build over time. Healthcare, in particular, can become a significant portion of retirement expenses, especially considering potential needs for long-term care. Investigating insurance options, potential medical needs, and lifestyle-related health choices can offer insights into the funds required. Meanwhile, understanding the cost of living in your desired retirement location enables better budgeting. For example, living in a metropolitan area might incur higher housing and utility costs compared to rural settings. By laying out these expected expenses clearly, retirees can develop a detailed picture of their needs, helping to avoid underestimations that could jeopardize financial stability later on.

Flexibility in adjusting your retirement goals ensures they remain aligned with changing circumstances. Life rarely follows a linear path, and dealing with unforeseen events is part of the journey. Whether it's alterations in income, unexpected medical emergencies, or shifts in life priorities, maintaining flexibility within your financial plans is crucial. For instance, being open to adjusting your retirement age by a few years, refining planned expenses, or modifying anticipated investments can mean the difference between success and shortfall in meeting retirement goals. This adaptability should be an integral part of your financial strategy, reducing the stress associated with sticking rigidly to outdated or unrealistic plans. Regularly revisiting and reassessing retirement plans allows individuals to make timely adjustments, keeping their goals both challenging and attainable.

Investment Strategies for Retirement Planning

Achieving financial stability in retirement hinges on well-planned investment strategies. By focusing on key areas such as diversification, tax-advantaged savings plans, portfolio understanding, and regular rebalancing, individuals can maximize growth potential leading up to retirement.

To begin with, strategic diversification stands as a cornerstone of any robust investment strategy. Diversification involves spreading investments across various asset classes to minimize risk while maximizing returns. This principle helps safeguard against the volatility of individual assets by ensuring that no single investment overly influences the portfolio. An effectively diversified portfolio may include a mix of stocks, bonds, real estate, and alternative investments like commodities or mutual funds. For example, stocks tend to offer higher growth potential, while bonds contribute stability. Real estate can provide both income and appreciation, acting as a hedge against inflation (Cussen, 2023). For younger investors, focusing more heavily on equities could be advantageous, given their longer time horizon to weather market fluctuations. Conversely, those closer to retirement might lean towards more stable investments to protect accumulated wealth.

Additionally, utilizing tax-advantaged retirement vehicles is essential for optimizing savings. Accounts like 401(k)s and IRAs allow individuals to grow their money tax-deferred, meaning taxes are paid upon withdrawal during retirement when individuals typically fall into a lower tax bracket. A traditional 401(k) plan, often employer-sponsored, allows contributions to be made pre-tax, reducing taxable income (Williams, 2023). Similarly, an Individual Retirement Account (IRA) offers opportunities for tax deductions depending on income level and filing status. Roth IRAs, conversely, involve after-tax contributions but allow tax-free withdrawals, providing significant advantages if taxes increase over time. These programs not only help in accumulating savings efficiently but also serve as accountability mechanisms, encouraging regular contributions through structured deposits.

Understanding the various types of investments is crucial in building a portfolio that supports long-term retirement goals. Stocks, renowned for their impressive returns over long periods, represent shares in a company's equity and embody a claim on its profits. Historically, equities have been a primary driver of wealth creation due to their capacity for growth, albeit with increased risk. Real estate investments, on the other hand, present opportunities for passive income generation and capital appreciation. They can diversify portfolios, as property values do not always move in tandem with stock markets. Real estate investment trusts (REITs) offer a practical means to invest in property without the challenges of direct ownership (Cussen, 2023). Exploring different investment avenues allows one to balance growth aspirations with risk tolerance, creating a resilient portfolio capable of navigating economic shifts.

Regular portfolio rebalancing is another critical practice in maintaining alignment with evolving retirement objectives. As market conditions fluctuate, portfolios can drift away from their intended allocation, skewing the risk profile. Regularly reviewing and adjusting the proportion of stocks, bonds, and other assets ensures that the investment strategy remains consistent with one's risk tolerance and retirement timeline. For instance, if a portfolio becomes too heavy in equities following a stock market surge, reallocating some funds into bonds or cash can restore balance. Rebalancing provides an opportunity to lock in gains in over-performing assets and reinvest them in underperforming ones, effectively benefiting from the market cycles (Williams, 2023). Additionally, setting a schedule—annually or semi-annually—or establishing a deviation threshold can guide when rebalancing should occur, reinforcing disciplined investing practices.

For young professionals seeking financial independence and middle-aged individuals planning for retirement, these investment strategies offer a pathway to securing future prosperity. By integrating diversified asset allocations, leveraging tax-efficient accounts, understanding diverse investment types, and committing to regular portfolio assessments, one can cultivate a dynamic financial foundation. Entrepreneurs, too, can benefit by broadening their financial portfolios beyond business operations, establishing multiple income streams to support ongoing ventures and personal goals.

Transitioning to Retirement Effectively

Embarking on the journey from active employment to retirement is a significant life transition that requires both financial planning and emotional readiness. To ensure this transition is as smooth as possible, developing a detailed retirement budget is pivotal. This budget acts as the framework for managing income sources such as pensions, social security, and investments while balancing them against your expected expenses. To effectively create this budget, start by listing all possible income streams. Consider not only your pension or social security but also any additional savings, part-time work, or passive income you may have. Next, categorize your expected expenses. Include essentials like housing, healthcare, and daily living costs, as well as discretionary spending such as travel and hobbies.

Creating this comprehensive budget isn't just about covering costs; it's about ensuring that your finances align with your lifestyle goals in retirement. A clear understanding of these elements allows you to identify areas where adjustments might be needed, perhaps reallocating funds or scaling back certain expenditures to maintain financial health. This process of budgeting provides peace of mind, giving a structure to your financial situation in retirement and allowing you to fully enjoy this new chapter without stress over monetary concerns.

In addition to financial preparations, acknowledging and preparing for potential emotional challenges is equally crucial. Retirement represents a shift not only in routine but in identity. The predictability and purpose provided by daily employment can leave a void when work concludes. Understanding this change is key to managing the emotional challenges it presents. Many individuals, upon retiring, encounter feelings of loss or uncertainty about their place and purpose. Before retiring, take time to reflect on what this stage means personally. Engage in conversations with retirees and gather insights on their experiences. Their stories can offer valuable perspectives and prepare you emotionally for what's ahead.

Transitioning into post-retirement activities plays a vital role in maintaining engagement and purpose. Volunteering is one particularly enriching option, providing opportunities to apply skills and contribute meaningfully to causes you care about. Whether it's tutoring, community gardening, or supporting local organizations, volunteering fulfills the need for connection and achievement beyond the workplace. Additionally, pursuing new hobbies or interests can further enrich your retirement experience. Exploring creative endeavors, joining clubs or groups, or even traveling are avenues that can bring joy and satisfaction. Engaging in new activities promotes mental sharpness and keeps boredom at bay, fostering a sense of accomplishment and enhanced well-being.

Furthermore, a structured retirement plan with regular reviews ensures personal fulfillment throughout this phase. Regularly reviewing your plans and goals adapts them to changing circumstances and evolving aspirations. This ongoing process lets you adjust your approach as necessary, keeping your retirement life vibrant and goal-oriented. Schedule periodic checks, perhaps annually or semi-annually, to evaluate whether you are meeting your financial and personal milestones. This ensures that your plans remain aligned with your current desires and any shifts in lifestyle or family dynamics.

Being proactive in this way prevents stagnation and supports continuous growth and engagement in retirement. It encourages an adaptive mindset, ready to embrace new opportunities or confront unexpected challenges without hesitation. By integrating flexibility into your plan, you're able to navigate the inevitable changes that come with aging, be they health-related or lifestyle-driven.

Adjusting Retirement Plans Over Time

Revisiting and modifying retirement goals as life circumstances change is a fundamental aspect of successful financial planning. Life is unpredictable, with various personal milestones, career shifts, economic changes, and unexpected challenges potentially impacting your financial landscape. Therefore, regularly revisiting these goals ensures that your plans remain relevant and effective, aligning not only with external economic conditions but also with evolving personal circumstances.

Regular evaluations are essential in keeping your retirement plans aligned with current changes in income and personal priorities. For instance, receiving a promotion or changing jobs might alter your income level significantly. Such changes offer an opportunity to increase your contributions towards your retirement savings, allowing for greater compound growth over time. Conversely, job loss or reduction in income may require a temporary scaling back on savings, which can be adjusted once stability returns. Regularly reviewing your retirement plans during annual financial assessments, or after significant life events, helps ensure that your savings strategy remains aligned with your updated financial picture.

Adapting to unforeseen financial challenges is crucial, and maintaining flexibility within your financial goals allows you to navigate bumps along the road without derailing long-term objectives. Unforeseen expenses, such as medical emergencies or sudden home repairs, can have significant impacts on planned savings. Building flexibility into your retirement plan means setting aside emergency funds and periodically adjusting your goals to accommodate such contingencies. Having these adaptable strategies can mitigate potential stress and prevent hasty financial decisions in times of crisis.

Adjusting timelines and milestones is another key component that enhances long-term financial security. As you progress through different stages of life, your timeline for reaching certain financial goals may shift. This could be due to changes in personal aspirations, such as deciding to retire earlier than initially planned or extending your work life. Adjustments might also arise from macroeconomic factors like inflation rates affecting purchasing power, thereby requiring a recalibration of expected retirement income needs. By being open to extending or shortening timelines based on real-world conditions and personal preferences, you ensure a more robust financial plan that supports ongoing stability and comfort.

Continuous engagement with retirement plans prevents feelings of stagnation or failure by encouraging proactive involvement in shaping one's financial future. A static approach to retirement planning can lead to feelings of disillusionment when initial goals seem out of reach. Instead, actively engaging with your retirement plans by tracking progress, celebrating small victories, and making necessary tweaks fosters a sense of accomplishment and motivation. This continuous adaptation transforms planning from a daunting task to an empowering journey where each step forward reinforces commitment to achieving a prosperous retirement.

Guidelines for implementing these adaptive measures include setting regular calendar reminders for financial reviews, incorporating both short-term and long-term goals within your retirement strategy, and cultivating a habit of saving that accommodates the ebb and flow of life's monetary demands. Above all, understanding that retirement planning is an evolving process rather than a fixed destination can empower individuals to make informed financial decisions throughout their lives.

The significance of reevaluating retirement goals cannot be understated, especially when considering how critical financial security is upon leaving the workforce. The emphasis on regular evaluations is not merely about micro-managing finances; rather, it's about creating a dynamic framework that thrives amidst life's unpredictability (Ng, 2024). Factors such as market volatility, changes in tax laws, and personal health shifts necessitate a responsive retirement strategy (Guillen, 2024). Engaging with these considerations consistently positions you ahead, ensuring readiness for future uncertainties while simultaneously capitalizing on opportunities.

Concluding Thoughts

In this chapter, we've explored the importance of setting clear retirement goals tailored to individual aspirations. Understanding where you want to be and what lifestyle you wish to lead in retirement forms the foundation of effective financial planning. By visualizing your dream future, you can identify necessary steps and approximate costs, creating a roadmap that translates abstract desires into achievable plans. Whether it's determining a target retirement age or estimating healthcare and living expenses, these considerations guide crucial decisions about savings and investments. Remember, flexibility remains vital as life evolves. Regularly reassessing and adapting your goals ensures they continue to align with your current circumstances.

The journey to securing a comfortable retirement is marked by strategic financial choices and a proactive mindset. Through diversification of investment strategies, utilizing tax-advantaged accounts, and maintaining an adaptable approach, you can build a robust financial portfolio that withstands life's unpredictabilities. By balancing risk and growth potential, young professionals, middle-aged planners, and entrepreneurs alike can work towards financial independence and longevity. Embarking on this path requires dedication and openness to adjustments, but it culminates in a financially stable and fulfilling retirement. Keep revisiting your plans, celebrating milestones, and adjusting as needed to stay on track for a prosperous future.

Reference List

A five-dimensional framework for retirement income needs and solutions | T. Rowe Price . (2024). Troweprice.com. https://www.troweprice.com/institutional/us/en/insights/articles/2024/q2/a-five-dimensional-framework-for-retirement-income-needs-and-solutions-na.html

Cussen, M. P. (2023, July 20). *How to Build an Investment Portfolio for Retirement* . Investopedia. https://www.investopedia.com/articles/financial-advisors/072915/what-does-ideal-retirement-portfolio-look.asp

Guillen, G. (2024, May 28). *Secure Your Future: The Importance of Starting Retirement Planning Now - UNCLE Credit Union* . UNCLE Credit Union. https://www.unclecu.org/secure-your-future/

Journey Through the Six Stages of Retirement . (2019). Investopedia. https://www.investopedia.com/articles/retirement/07/sixstages.asp

Ng, D. (2024, April 25). *10 Reasons Why Retirement Planning is Important & Must-Know Tips for 2024* . Churchill. https://

www.churchillmanagement.com/why-retirement-planning-is-important/

Thrivent. (2024, March 7). *5 Simple Retirement Planning Questions to Ask Yourself | Thrivent* . Thrivent.com. https://www.thrivent.com/insights/retirement-planning/5-questions-to-ask-yourself-during-retirement-planning

Williams, R. (2023, July 11). *Structuring Your Retirement Portfolio* . Schwab Brokerage. https://www.schwab.com/learn/story/structuring-your-retirement-portfolio

What To Expect When Retiring: The Six Phases of Retirement . (2024). Carrolladvisory.com. https://www.carrolladvisory.com/blog/what-to-expect-when-retiring-the-six-phases-of-retirement

Chapter 8

Tools and Techniques for Smart Investments

Investing wisely involves employing the right tools and techniques to foster financial growth. In a world where financial management is increasingly intertwined with technological advancements, the landscape of investment has transformed dramatically. Today, individuals have unprecedented access to resources that can streamline their investment efforts, allowing them to make informed decisions with greater ease. The convenience of technology has redefined how people approach investing, breaking down barriers that once hindered many from participating in the market.

This chapter delves into the various tools and innovative strategies that can enhance one's financial journey. Readers will explore the diverse functionalities of investment apps, which have made trading more accessible than ever before. The advantages of real-time data and automated features will be highlighted, showcasing how these elements assist both beginners and seasoned investors alike. Additionally, the chapter will cover the role of budgeting software in managing personal finances and maintaining control over expenses. Robo-advisors, which offer tailored investment plans at affordable fees, will also be discussed as they democratize portfolio management. Furthermore, online brokerage platforms, with their commission-free trades and wealth of educational resources, expand investment opportunities for everyone. With insights into these dynamic aspects, readers will gain a comprehensive understanding of how to navigate the modern investment landscape effectively.

Using Technology for Financial Management

In today's rapidly evolving financial landscape, technology plays a pivotal role in streamlining financial management, making it more accessible and efficient for individuals to track and optimize their investments. One of the most transformative innovations in this realm is the advent of investment apps. These applications have revolutionized the way people engage with the stock market by simplifying trading processes, providing real-time data, and offering an array of automated features that cater to both novice and experienced investors.

Investment apps are designed to make the trading process straightforward and user-friendly. Gone are the days when individuals needed to call brokers or navigate complex interfaces to execute trades. Now, with just a few taps on their smartphones, users can buy and sell stocks, monitor their portfolio's performance, and stay updated with the latest market trends. This ease of use empowers individuals from all walks of life to take charge of their financial future without being bogged down by technical barriers.

Moreover, these apps provide real-time data feeds that keep users informed of market changes as they happen. Timely notifications about price fluctuations, earnings reports, and other crucial financial events ensure that investors can adjust their strategies promptly. This level of access to information was once reserved for professional traders and affluent investors, but now anyone with a smartphone can leverage these insights to make informed decisions.

Automated features further enhance the appeal of investment apps. Many apps offer automation tools such as recurring investments, portfolio rebalancing, and tax optimization strategies. For example, users can set up automatic investments into specific stocks or index funds, ensuring consistent contributions to their portfolios without manual intervention. Portfolio rebalancing helps maintain the desired asset allocation by automatically adjusting holdings based on predefined criteria, thus removing the emotional biases that often affect investor behavior.

Another technological tool that has profoundly impacted financial management is budgeting software. For those aiming to gain control over their expenses, budgeting software offers a digital solution that replaces traditional pen-and-paper methods. These programs allow users to track their spending effortlessly by categorizing transactions and linking directly to bank accounts and credit cards. As expenses are logged automatically, individuals can easily visualize where their money is going and identify areas where they might rein in their spending.

Budgeting software often includes insightful visual tools such as graphs and charts that illustrate spending habits over time. By analyzing these visuals, users can gain a deeper understanding of their financial patterns and make more informed

Personal Finance Strategies

choices about saving and investing. Additionally, these programs can set up reminders for upcoming bills or savings goals, keeping users on track to meet their financial objectives. This structured approach to personal finance management supports both short-term and long-term planning, allowing individuals to cultivate healthier financial habits.

Robo-advisors present another technological advancement that has democratized investment management. Offering personalized plans and automated portfolio rebalancing at low fees, robo-advisors combine algorithmic expertise with cost efficiency. By assessing an individual's financial goals, risk tolerance, and time horizon, these platforms tailor investment strategies that align with the user's unique profile. The hands-off nature of robo-advisors means that even inexperienced investors can benefit from sophisticated portfolio management without having to actively manage their investments.

Automation is at the core of what makes robo-advisors so appealing. They continuously monitor market conditions and adjust portfolios to maintain optimal asset allocation. This ensures that users' investments remain balanced between risk and reward while minimizing human error or emotional decision-making. Furthermore, low fees associated with robo-advisors reduce the cost barrier often associated with traditional advisory services, making them accessible to a wider range of investors.

Online brokerage platforms also play a crucial role in expanding access to diverse investment opportunities. Unlike conventional brokerages, which may have high entry barriers or transaction fees, many online platforms offer commission-free trades, lowering the cost of entry for new investors. This affordability encourages individuals to explore a broader spectrum of investment options, from stocks and bonds to exchange-traded funds (ETFs) and cryptocurrencies.

These platforms empower users with a wealth of resources to make informed investment choices. Research tools, educational content, and interactive dashboards help investors analyze potential investments and understand how diverse assets fit into their financial goals. By breaking down information silos and reducing costs, online brokerage platforms make it possible for individuals to construct well-rounded portfolios that align with their objectives.

For those utilizing budgeting software, setting clear guidelines can further enhance financial management. Establishing categories for different types of expenses (such as groceries, entertainment, and transportation) allows users to allocate their budget effectively and prevents overspending in any given area. Regularly reviewing these categories and adjusting allocations based on changing needs or priorities enables more dynamic financial planning. Additionally, aligning budgets with long-term goals—such as saving for retirement or building an emergency fund—ensures that day-to-day spending aligns with broader financial aspirations.

Analyzing Investment Opportunities

In the realm of smart investments, conducting a thorough analysis is pivotal before committing to any opportunity. This process begins with fundamental analysis, where investors delve into a company's financial health to evaluate its intrinsic value. Fundamental analysis involves examining financial statements such as income statements, balance sheets, and cash flow statements. Through these documents, analysts look at metrics like revenues, profits, and operating expenses to determine whether a company is undervalued or overvalued in the market. This method allows investors to discern the true value of a company beyond market fluctuations. Prominent investors, including Warren Buffett, have long championed this approach, seeking stocks whose market price is lower than their intrinsic worth (Twin, 2019).

As we shift from fundamental analysis, technical analysis provides another layer of insight by focusing on chart patterns and historical data. Technical analysts rely heavily on statistical tools, graphs, and historical price data to predict future market movements. This method is favored by day traders who scan the short-term movements indicated by trends and patterns. By analyzing these charts, investors can make informed decisions about the timing of their trades. Recognizing patterns like "head and shoulders" or moving averages aids in anticipating market shifts. Unlike fundamental analysis, which assesses intrinsic value, technical analysis looks purely at market data to project future prices (Segal, 2024).

Industry analysis is equally crucial as it considers economic cycles and sector performance to identify prevailing trends. By understanding the broader industry context, investors can foresee potential growth or decline cycles that could impact investments. For example, during periods of economic expansion, certain sectors like technology may thrive, while others might lag. Conversely, in an economic downturn, consumer staples might outperform other industries due to consistent demand. Industry analysis helps investors align their portfolios with sectors poised for growth, ensuring they are well-positioned for impending market changes.

A comprehensive investment analysis also incorporates risk assessment. Identifying potential risks associated with investment opportunities is critical to safeguarding against significant losses. Risk assessment doesn't just involve recognizing potential financial pitfalls; it extends to evaluating political, economic, and industry-specific threats that could affect an investment's outcome. Through diversification, investors can mitigate these risks. Diversification spreads investments across various asset classes, reducing the impact of poor performance in any single area. By doing so, investors can shield themselves from volatility and enhance portfolio stability.

Guidelines for conducting these analyses effectively can be beneficial. For fundamental analysis, it is important to focus on key financial ratios such as the price-to-earnings ratio, return on equity, and debt-to-equity ratio. These figures provide snapshots of a company's valuation, profitability, and leverage. In technical analysis, paying attention to moving averages, resistance levels, and volume indicators can help identify optimal entry and exit points. When performing industry analysis, review cyclical indicators and growth forecasts to gauge sector performance. Meanwhile, in risk assessment, diversify investments across both domestic and international markets and consider including different asset types like equities, bonds, and real estate to cushion against unforeseen market turbulence.

Although each type of analysis offers unique insights, they are most powerful when used together. A meticulous combination of fundamental, technical, and industry analysis, coupled with thorough risk assessment, equips investors with a holistic view of potential opportunities. This multi-pronged approach ensures that investments are not only based on solid data but are also aligned with broader market conditions. Moreover, by acknowledging the limitations and challenges inherent in each method —such as the time-consuming nature of fundamental analysis or the subjective interpretation required for technical analysis— investors can make better-informed, balanced decisions.

Understanding Market Trends

Recognizing and interpreting market trends is an essential skill for anyone aiming to make strategic investment decisions. It serves as a compass in the ever-changing landscape of financial markets, where various factors influence potential outcomes for investors. By understanding these dynamics, one can position themselves advantageously, be it for long-term growth or seizing short-term opportunities.

A pivotal component of understanding market conditions lies in grasping economic indicators such as gross domestic product (GDP) and interest rates. These indicators offer a window into the broader economic environment. GDP, which measures the total value of goods and services produced within a country, reflects the health and growth trajectory of an economy. A growing GDP generally signals robust corporate earnings and investor confidence, often leading to bullish market behaviors. Conversely, a declining GDP might flag recessionary pressures, prompting caution among investors. Interest rates, set by central banks, directly impact borrowing costs and consumer spending. Lower rates typically stimulate economic activity by making loans cheaper, fostering an expansionary phase. On the other hand, higher rates can cool down an overheating economy by increasing borrowing costs, thus affecting stock prices and bond yields. Understanding both GDP and interest rate trends aids investors in predicting market movements and adjusting their strategies accordingly (PIMCO, 2023).

Market sentiment, influenced significantly by investor psychology, is another critical factor in shaping market trends. This collective attitude towards market conditions is often driven by emotions like fear and greed, which can provoke irrational decision-making. Bullish sentiment typically indicates wide investor optimism, driving prices up as more individuals buy assets in anticipation of future gains. This was evident during the tech boom when optimism fueled soaring stock prices beyond fundamental valuations. In contrast, bearish sentiment reflects widespread pessimism, often resulting in sell-offs and declining asset values. For instance, during economic downturns, fear can lead to dramatic market drops as investors rush to liquidate holdings. Recognizing market sentiment helps investors anticipate price swings and adjust their portfolios to mitigate risks or capitalize on favorable trends (Allen, 2019).

Global news and events also play a substantial role in market volatility and can create ripple effects across financial markets. Political developments, natural disasters, and geopolitical tensions are examples of events that introduce volatility, impacting investor confidence and asset prices. For instance, Brexit uncertainties caused significant fluctuations in currency and stock markets as investors grappled with the potential implications for trade and economic stability. Similarly, natural disasters like hurricanes can disrupt supply chains and affect commodities, influencing everything from oil prices to agricultural outputs. Staying informed about global events enables investors to respond swiftly to these changes, safeguarding their assets against unexpected shifts and exploiting opportunities as they arise.

Emerging technologies present another layer of complexity and opportunity within market trends. Innovations such as artificial intelligence, blockchain, and renewable energy technologies are reshaping industries and creating new investment avenues. For example, the rise of electric vehicles has spurred substantial investments in lithium mining and battery technologies, reflecting shifting consumer preferences and regulatory pushes towards sustainability. Investors attuned to these technological advancements can identify disruptive forces poised to transform traditional markets, potentially offering lucrative returns. Understanding how these technologies integrate into existing frameworks is crucial for foreseeing industry shifts and capitalizing on new growth areas.

To navigate the multifaceted world of investments effectively, combining knowledge of economic indicators, market sentiment, global events, and emerging technologies is vital. Each element provides distinct insights that, when woven together, form a comprehensive view of market trends. For young professionals eager to escape the paycheck-to-paycheck cycle, this understanding facilitates strategic planning, empowering them to build secure financial futures through informed investments. Middle-aged individuals preparing for retirement can leverage these insights to safeguard their savings, ensuring their portfolios withstand market fluctuations and deliver sustained returns. Entrepreneurs striving to diversify income streams benefit from recognizing innovation-driven trends, enabling them to expand their financial portfolios judiciously.

Leveraging Diversification for Risk Management

In the world of smart investments, diversification stands out as a cornerstone strategy for managing risk effectively. The primary goal of diversification is to spread investment across various asset classes and sectors, which helps in reducing the overall risk faced by an investment portfolio. By investing in a diverse range of assets, investors mitigate the impact of poor performance in any single asset type, leading to more stable returns over time.

Diversification works on the principle that different asset classes often do not react identically to market forces. For instance, equities, bonds, real estate, and commodities might all respond differently to changes in interest rates or economic conditions. When one sector experiences a downturn, another might perform well or remain unaffected, thus balancing out the overall risk. This counterbalancing effect is crucial during economic shifts, where some sectors may surge while others plummet.

To illustrate this, consider an investor who has only invested in technology stocks. If a technological bubble bursts or there is a significant regulatory change against tech firms, this investor's entire portfolio could suffer severe losses. However, if this investor had also included healthcare, consumer goods, and energy stocks, the negative impact from the technology sector might be lessened by gains or stability in these other sectors.

Another dimension of diversification is geographic variety through international investments. Investing beyond domestic markets opens up opportunities in emerging economies or regions experiencing growth phases. International investments add a layer of geographic diversification that can further reduce risks associated with local economic downturns or political instability. For example, while a recession in the United States might affect American companies, it might have little or no impact on businesses operating primarily in Asia or Europe. These geographic disparities allow investors to tap into potential higher returns from flourishing global markets (Segal, 2023).

Additionally, investing internationally diversifies currency exposure, adding another layer of protection against currency depreciation in one's home country. Although international investments can introduce new elements like currency risk, they typically contribute to a portfolio's long-term robustness.

Leveraging diversified portfolios helps investors protect against volatility and enhances stability. Volatility, characterized by unpredictable swings in asset prices, can be unsettling, especially for novice investors or those nearing retirement. A well-diversified portfolio reduces sensitivity to such price fluctuations. Consider a portfolio balanced among high-risk/high-return assets such as stocks and more stable options like bonds or cash equivalents. While the stocks might offer high growth during bullish markets, bonds could stabilize the portfolio during bear markets or economic downturns.

Moreover, diversification allows for a flexible approach to invest based on personal financial goals and risk tolerance. Young professionals, eager to escape a paycheck-to-paycheck lifestyle, may blend growth-oriented domestic and international stocks with some safer, income-generating assets. Middle-aged individuals, focusing on retirement planning, might prioritize a combination of steady bond investments and select equities for growth.

Entrepreneurs looking to establish multiple income streams can benefit from diversification by exploring investments beyond their primary business ventures. They might put money into real estate, peer-to-peer lending, or alternative assets like cryptocurrencies, depending on their risk appetite and market knowledge (Lioudis, 2024).

A crucial aspect of diversification is understanding that while it reduces unsystematic risk—specific to individual companies or industries—it cannot eliminate systematic risk inherent to the market. Thus, while diversification significantly enhances a portfolio's defensive capabilities, it's essential for investors to continue monitoring market trends and adjust their strategies accordingly.

Adopting a diversified approach requires discipline and sometimes patience, as it may limit outsized gains from single successful investments. However, the trade-off is reduced exposure to devastating losses when a chosen investment fails. It is a protective measure that seeks to ensure consistent returns rather than extreme highs and lows.

Summary and Reflections

The chapter has explored how technology can significantly enhance financial management by providing accessible tools like investment apps, budgeting software, and robo-advisors. These innovations empower individuals across experience levels to take control of their financial futures. From easily managing trades through apps to automating portfolio adjustments with robo-advisors, the integration of real-time data and automation simplifies decision-making and reduces barriers to market participation. Budgeting software offers a clear view of personal spending, aiding in the formation of sustainable financial habits that align with long-term goals.

Furthermore, the role of online brokerage platforms and the importance of diversification have been highlighted as strategies for expanding and stabilizing investments. By offering commission-free trades and educational resources, these platforms lower entry costs and encourage diversified portfolios suited to individual financial objectives. Diversification across asset classes and geographical locations helps manage risk, ensuring a more secure financial foundation. Whether young professionals are looking to break free from financial constraints, middle-aged individuals are planning for retirement, or entrepreneurs are seeking new income streams, leveraging these technological tools and diversification strategies fosters a proactive approach to achieving financial growth.

Reference List

Allen, B. (2019). *Economic Indicators That Help Predict Market Trends* . Investopedia. https://www.investopedia.com/articles/economics/08/leading-economic-indicators.asp

Lioudis, N. (2024). *The Importance Of Diversification* . Investopedia. https://www.investopedia.com/investing/importance-diversification/

Piero Politeo. (2024, November 18). *How to use fintech tools to improve your investments | Exirio* . Exirio. https://www.exirio.com/how-to-use-fintech-tools-to-improve-your-investments/

PIMCO. (2023). *Learning the Significance of Key Economic Indicators | PIMCO* . Pacific Investment Management Company LLC. https://www.pimco.com/us/en/resources/education/learning-the-significance-of-key-economic-indicators

Segal, T. (2024, June 21). *Fundamental analysis: Principles, types, and how to use it* .

Investopedia. https://www.investopedia.com/terms/f/fundamentalanalysis.asp

Segal, T. (2023, July 1). *What Is Diversification? Definition as Investing Strategy* . Investopedia. https://www.investopedia.com/terms/d/diversification.asp

Twin, A. (2019). *Investment Analysis: The Key to Sound Portfolio Management Strategy* . Investopedia. https://www.investopedia.com/terms/i/investment-analysis.asp

Team, T. R. (2024, October 21). *Technology in Financial Services (Fintech): 10 Key Emerging Tools | Rippling* . Rippling. https://www.rippling.com/blog/technology-in-financial-services

Chapter 9

Success Stories: Learning from the Pros

Gaining insights from successful wealth builders can illuminate the pathways to financial success. The journeys of those who have successfully navigated towards prosperity provide invaluable lessons and inspiration, showing that multiple routes can lead to financial achievement. These narratives often highlight the blend of strategic foresight, calculated risks, and innovative thinking crucial for building substantial wealth. Observing how different individuals have succeeded not only enriches our understanding but also motivates us to explore diverse methods in pursuit of similar goals. By studying various success stories, we are reminded that wealth is not merely the result of luck or timing; it's the outcome of deliberate actions and informed decisions.

This chapter delves into a collection of compelling case studies involving entrepreneurs, real estate investors, stock market enthusiasts, and influencers who have transformed their ambitions into realities. With each story, readers are introduced to unique strategies tailored to specific industries and objectives. Whether it's fostering innovation within a tech startup, making calculated investments in properties and stocks, or leveraging personal branding in the digital age, these examples offer both practical guidance and aspirational insights. Through these narratives, the chapter aims to equip readers with the knowledge and

Personal Finance Strategies

confidence needed to carve their paths toward financial success, encouraging them to take informed steps inspired by proven successes.

Case Studies of Financial Success

Success stories are powerful tools for learning, especially when they reveal the thought processes and strategies behind financial triumphs. Let's explore real-life instances of individuals who reached their financial goals through diverse paths.

Take the inspiring journey of a young entrepreneur, who made innovation and rapid growth his cornerstones. By leveraging modern networking techniques and an insatiable appetite for continuous learning, he managed to transform a simple idea into a thriving business. He foresaw the potential in digital platforms, enhancing his reach significantly. This endless quest for knowledge allowed him to stay ahead of competitors, embracing new technologies faster, and adapting swiftly to changing market dynamics. His story illustrates how dedication to innovation can propel business growth exponentially.

In another success story, a couple embarked on a wealth-building journey through real estate. Their strategy was meticulous—meticulously scouting locations, analyzing market trends, and patiently waiting for opportune moments to invest. Over time, they honed their approach by understanding fluctuations in property values and demographics. Patience, as shown here, is often just as critical as sharp investment skills. This couple's ability to delay gratification and stick to a long-term plan underscores the power of steady, informed decision-making in accumulating wealth through real estate ventures.

The realm of stocks offers its path to prosperity, as demonstrated by an individual who crafted a robust stock portfolio. This person didn't rely on whims; instead, strategic stock picking became a hallmark of their success. They engaged in comprehensive analysis to understand company fundamentals and market conditions. Effective risk management played a key role in protecting assets, while a vision oriented towards long-term gains ensured that short-term market volatility didn't derail their overall financial aspirations. This approach highlights how disciplined investment strategies can yield significant financial returns over time.

Finally, we look at an influencer who morphed into an entrepreneur, showcasing the transformative power of authenticity and strategic partnerships. Initially recognized for their engaging online presence, this individual tapped into their influence to create a sustainable business model. Authenticity proved invaluable, as it bred trust and a loyal following. By forming strategic collaborations with like-minded partners, the influencer expanded their enterprise, demonstrating that personal branding can lay the foundation for flourishing businesses.

These diverse stories, sourced from everyday innovators and investors, provide rich insights into the varied avenues leading to financial success. Each narrative emphasizes unique elements—be it relentless innovation, methodical planning, patient strategy, or authentic engagement—that contributed essential pieces to their respective puzzles of wealth building. As such, these examples serve both as inspirations and practical guides for those eager to master the art of financial growth in their lives.

By examining these stories, one can glean important lessons about the necessity of tailored strategies and the importance of maintaining a flexible mindset. Success is rarely linear; it requires adaptation, perseverance, and a keen understanding of one's chosen path. Whether it's the calculated risks taken in entrepreneurship, the diligent research conducted in real estate investments, the strategic choices made in stock portfolios, or the effective use of personal influence, each path holds valuable teachings on achieving financial aspirations.

Lessons from Failures and How to Avoid Them

In the world of finance and investment, cautionary tales serve as invaluable lessons for those eager to build wealth without falling prey to common pitfalls. These stories illuminate what can go wrong despite the best intentions, offering insights into how one might navigate the complex terrain of financial management.

Consider the case of an investor who neglected thorough research before diving into a high-risk venture. Initially drawn by the promise of rapid gains, the investor allowed emotions and the thrill of potential success to override rational decision-making. The outcome was significant financial loss, which could have been mitigated through diversification—a fundamental principle in investing that advocates spreading investments across various assets to reduce risk. Emotionally driven decisions, particularly ones made under pressure or influenced by market hype, often bypass critical analysis. This example underscores the necessity of due diligence and objective evaluation when making investment choices, as well as the importance of not letting emotions dictate actions.

Another illustrative tale involves a real estate developer who fell into the trap of over-leveraging. Enthralled by the booming housing market, the developer took on excessive debt to expand holdings rapidly, expecting continuous upward market trends. However, when economic conditions shifted, the heavy debt burden became unsustainable, leading to severe financial repercussions. This situation highlights the pivotal role of cash flow management in sustaining financial health. It educates readers on conservative financing strategies, emphasizing the need to balance ambition with pragmatism. Managing debt wisely and planning for contingencies can safeguard against unforeseen downturns and ensure long-term viability.

An entrepreneur's experience further exemplifies the perils of neglecting market alignment. Launching a business requires not only innovation but also an acute awareness of consumer needs and preferences. In this case, the entrepreneur failed to adapt to evolving market demands and ignored critical feedback from consumers. The inability to pivot quickly in response to changing conditions led to diminishing returns and eventually, business stagnation. This story serves as a lesson in maintaining flexibility within business strategies. Entrepreneurs must remain attuned to their audience, ready to adjust offerings, marketing approaches, and operational

Personal Finance Strategies

tactics based on constructive feedback and market shifts.

Similarly, the tale of a stock trader overwhelmed by the urge for revenge trading sheds light on the psychological challenges in wealth building. After experiencing a string of losses, the trader attempted to recover lost funds through aggressive trading strategies, abandoning careful analysis in favor of rash decisions aimed at immediate recovery. This cycle fed into further losses, illustrating the destructive nature of reacting impulsively to setbacks. The importance of adhering to a pre-established plan is evident here, as is the value of taking strategic pauses to reassess one's approach objectively. Learning to recognize when to step back and reflect can prevent compounding mistakes and facilitate more calculated, effective decision-making.

These cautionary tales encapsulate a shared theme: the balance between ambition and caution. While ambition drives individuals toward financial growth, unbridled enthusiasm without strategic foresight can lead to detrimental outcomes. Each story demonstrates that awareness, adaptability, and emotional discipline are crucial components in mastering wealth accumulation. Wealth builders are encouraged to integrate these lessons into their financial practices, ensuring that their paths to prosperity are supported by thoughtful planning and informed choices.

By drawing upon these examples, readers can better understand how successful individuals navigate the complexities of financial landscapes, leveraging knowledge gained from others' experiences to sidestep similar missteps. Each narrative reinforces the overarching message that while the journey to wealth is paved with opportunities, it is equally fraught with risks that demand vigilance, adaptability, and mindful management. Whether one is just starting their financial journey or looking to refine existing strategies, these stories offer essential lessons for constructing a solid foundation for enduring wealth.

Drawing conclusions from these cautionary narratives empowers individuals to engage with their finances more thoughtfully. They highlight the importance of learning from past mistakes and adopting flexible, responsive strategies. Whether addressing the need for diversification, managing debt prudently, aligning with market dynamics, or adhering to a disciplined approach in volatile circumstances, the insights gleaned from these tales guide readers toward more secure and prosperous futures. Such wisdom is indispensable for anyone seeking to transcend the paycheck-to-paycheck cycle, prepare effectively for retirement, or explore entrepreneurial avenues for expanding income streams. Understanding and applying these lessons equips individuals to make informed decisions that enhance financial stability and success.

Adopting Strategies from Successful Investors

In today's fast-paced financial landscape, adopting strategies from successful investors is more crucial than ever for building wealth. One such strategy that stands out is the long-term investment philosophy, which advocates for patience, compounding returns, and setting clear financial goals. Imagine your investments as seeds. Over time, with care and attention, these seeds grow into a lush forest. This forest isn't built overnight but through consistent nurturing over many years. Patience allows investors to ride out market fluctuations without succumbing to the panic of selling during downturns. The power of compounding returns cannot be overstated. By reinvesting earnings, even small initial amounts can grow significantly over time. Setting clear financial goals acts as a compass, guiding investment decisions and keeping investors focused on their long-term objectives (Noonan, 2019).

Continuous education and market analysis form another pillar of successful investing. The financial world is dynamic and constantly evolving. Staying informed about the latest trends and developments helps investors make better decisions. Utilizing available resources, such as financial news outlets and reputable online courses, equips individuals with the knowledge they need to navigate changing market landscapes. Additionally, seeking mentorship and expert advice provides invaluable insights from those who have already succeeded in the industry. Learning from experienced investors can illuminate pitfalls to avoid and highlight profitable opportunities ripe for the taking (Paulus, 2023).

Risk management is yet another critical component. Investing always carries a level of risk, but managing this risk effectively can mean the difference between success and failure. Hedging against potential losses involves diversifying investments across various asset classes to buffer the impact of any single loss. Balancing asset allocation ensures that no single investment dominates the portfolio, reducing exposure to negative market movements. Moreover, maintaining a financial safety net—such as emergency savings—provides a cushion against unforeseen expenses or economic downturns. This buffer gives investors peace of mind and the confidence to pursue long-term strategies without fear of immediate financial ruin (Paulus, 2023).

Networking with like-minded individuals is an often overlooked strategy but one that can yield substantial benefits. Building a network of investors and professionals creates opportunities for collaboration and innovation. Through connections, individuals can access new information, gain fresh perspectives, and find motivation from peers facing similar challenges. A supportive community fosters sharing of experiences and best practices, enriching everyone's journey towards wealth accumulation. Networking can open doors to partnerships and ventures that might otherwise remain inaccessible, further expanding one's financial portfolio.

To adopt these proven strategies, consider the following guidelines:

Long-term Investment Philosophy:

1. Cultivate patience by focusing on long-term goals and avoiding knee-jerk reactions to short-term market changes.

2. Harness the power of compounding by reinvesting dividends and interest.

3. Set specific, measurable, achievable, relevant, and time-bound (SMART) financial goals to ensure a clear path forward (Noonan, 2019).

Continuous Education and Market Analysis:

1. Stay abreast of industry news and emerging market trends.

2. Leverage online resources and courses to enhance knowledge.
3. Seek mentors or financial advisors who provide guidance based on experience and expertise (Paulus, 2023).

Risk Management Techniques:

1. Diversify investments to spread risk across different sectors and asset types.
2. Balance your portfolio regularly to align with your risk tolerance and financial goals.
3. Maintain an emergency fund to mitigate unexpected financial burdens (Paulus, 2023).

Networking with Like-minded Individuals:

1. Join investment clubs or forums to connect with peers and industry experts.
2. Attend seminars and webinars to meet professionals and expand your circle.
3. Engage in meaningful conversations that inspire and challenge your thinking.

Diverse Paths to Wealth

In the pursuit of building wealth, it is crucial to recognize the diversity in available paths. Each journey has its unique set of strategies and potential risks, informed by personal interests, market knowledge, and economic trends. By examining various case studies, we unravel how entrepreneurs, investors, and influencers have effectively transformed their ventures into substantial sources of wealth.

Innovation and entrepreneurship often serve as a powerful catalyst for scaling businesses swiftly and effectively. Consider the journey of a tech startup that began with a simple idea but grew exponentially due to innovative solutions and strategic networking. For instance, leveraging technology to address consumer needs can create rapid growth opportunities. Entrepreneurs like Elon Musk, with ventures such as SpaceX and Tesla, exemplify the impact of combining innovation with entrepreneurship. By focusing on future technologies and sustainable solutions, Musk's businesses challenged industry norms, attracting massive investments and driving significant value creation. Such examples highlight the importance of continuous learning, adaptability, and resilience in navigating entrepreneurial waters.

Simultaneously, real estate remains a tried-and-true vehicle for wealth generation. Engaging in methodical property investment requires understanding market trends, demographic shifts, and economic forecasts. Successful investors use this knowledge to buy undervalued properties, improve them, and sell or rent them at a profit. One notable example is Grant Cardone, who built his wealth through astute real estate acquisitions. Cardone capitalized on market downturns, purchasing multi-family units at lower prices, and held them for long-term appreciation and steady cash flow. This approach underscores the importance of patience, strategic planning, and leveraging cyclical market conditions to maximize returns over time.

Stock portfolios represent another avenue for wealth accumulation, demanding strategic selections and a disciplined, long-term outlook. Building a robust portfolio typically involves diversifying assets across sectors to mitigate risk and capture growth opportunities. The success story of Warren Buffett epitomizes this strategy, as he has consistently advocated for investing in fundamentally strong companies with fair valuations. His philosophy emphasizes compounding returns and unwavering commitment to long-term investing principles. This method highlights the significance of research, emotional stability, and the wisdom of not chasing short-term gains at the expense of financial health.

Additionally, the realm of social media and personal branding has opened new doors for turning influence into entrepreneurial success. Many influencers have transitioned from being content creators to business owners by harnessing authenticity and forming strategic partnerships. Take the example of Huda Kattan, who transformed her beauty blog into a billion-dollar cosmetics brand, Huda Beauty. By engaging authentically with her audience and collaborating with leading makeup artists and retailers, she created a trusted brand identity and captured a loyal customer base. This transformation reflects the power of leveraging personal influence to foster community trust and drive business growth.

Each path illustrates varied but complementary strategies towards achieving financial independence. While innovation fuels rapid business expansion, real estate offers a steadier, more predictable avenue for wealth building. Stock portfolios require rigorous analysis and patience, whereas personal branding combines creativity with commerce. What these paths share is the necessity for clear goals, thorough market understanding, and an ability to adapt to changing environments.

Moreover, these examples emphasize the need for strategic planning and risk management. Whether it's mitigating investment risks in stocks or ensuring liquidity in real estate, successful wealth builders prioritize protecting their gains while pursuing growth. They also exhibit a relentless commitment to self-improvement, always seeking knowledge and expanding their networks for better opportunities.

Ultimately, wealth building is not a one-size-fits-all endeavor. It requires an alignment of personal strengths, passion, and market dynamics. Aspiring wealth builders should explore various avenues, considering factors such as initial investment requirements, time commitment, and personal risk tolerance. By studying diverse success stories, individuals can craft personalized strategies that resonate with their goals and aspirations.

Concluding Thoughts

As we've explored in this chapter, each story of financial success offers invaluable insights into distinct strategies that can lead to significant wealth accumulation. From the innovative young entrepreneur harnessing digital platforms for business growth, to the patient and analytical couple triumphing in real estate, these narratives underscore the importance of embracing a strategy tailored to one's strengths and goals. Whether it's through disciplined investment choices in the stock market or leveraging personal influence like the influencer turned entrepreneur, the stories serve as both inspiration and practical guidance for those seeking to navigate their financial journeys.

By reflecting on these diverse paths, readers are encouraged to recognize that while no two journeys are identical, fundamental principles like innovation, patience, strategic planning, and authenticity consistently emerge as critical components of success. These examples remind us that mastering financial growth requires more than just luck; it demands dedication, adaptability, and a deep understanding of one's chosen path. Whether starting out or refining existing strategies, young professionals, those planning for retirement, and entrepreneurs alike can draw valuable lessons from these case studies, equipping themselves with the knowledge and skills necessary to build a secure and prosperous future.

Reference List

Cote, C. (2022, January 20). *4 Entrepreneur Success Stories to Learn From | HBS Online* . Business Insights Blog. https://online.hbs.edu/blog/post/successful-entrepreneur-stories

Cohen, S. S. (2024, September 14). *4 Real Life Story Examples of Successful Investment Strategies* . GOBankingRates. https://www.gobankingrates.com/investing/strategy/real-life-story-examples-of-successful-investment-strategies/

Case Study . (2024, October 4). Wharton Global Youth Program. https://

globalyouth.wharton.upenn.edu/competitions/investment-competition/case-study/

Koshy, S. (2022, September 20). *Manifest Diversity and the Empire of Finance* . Post45: Peer Reviewed. https://post45.org/2022/09/manifest-diversity-and-the-empire-of-finance/

LibGuides: Financial Literacy in Public Libraries: A Guide for Building Collections: Books . (2024). Ala.org. https://libguides.ala.org/finra-ore/personalfinance/books

Noonan, K. (2019, November 17). *Investment Strategies for the Long Term* . The Motley Fool. https://www.fool.com/investing/how-to-invest/stocks/investment-strategies/

Paulus, N. (2023, December 5). *Guide to Long-Term Investment Strategies* . MoneyGeek.com. https://doi.org/10116477/81e3ed8b0af0404181ed7280bce15ecf

Yik, H. (2016, June). *3 innovative approaches to investment, from industry experts* . World Economic Forum. https://www.weforum.org/stories/2016/06/3-innovative-approaches-to-investment-from-industry-experts/

Chapter 10

Mindset Shifts for Wealth Building

Building wealth requires a mindset shift that aligns with financial success. While strategies and techniques are essential, the mental approach to money is often what differentiates those who thrive financially from those who struggle. This chapter dives into how psychological barriers can impede progress, making it crucial to identify and challenge any limiting beliefs you may hold. As readers explore the content, they will find insights into recognizing these mental obstacles and steps to transform them to support their financial journey.

The chapter offers practical strategies and real-life scenarios to help readers embrace new ways of thinking about money. By examining personal narratives and societal influences, this section guides individuals in pinpointing the roots of their financial mindsets, which often stem from childhood experiences or ingrained cultural norms. It goes on to suggest innovative reframing techniques, including visualization and affirmations, that can help change negative perceptions into empowering stories about money. Additionally, the chapter highlights the importance of seeking external support through networks and communities that encourage a positive view of wealth-building. By blending introspective exercises with actionable advice, this chapter lays the groundwork for a deeper understanding of how mindset influences financial outcomes, encouraging readers to cultivate a perspective that not only accepts but actively pursues financial growth.

Overcoming Psychological Barriers to Wealth

Cultivating a mindset conducive to financial success involves understanding and identifying the mental blocks that can hinder your ability to build wealth. These mental blocks, often referred to as limiting beliefs, can be deeply embedded in our subconscious and significantly impact how we view and manage money.

One of the first steps to overcoming these barriers is recognizing limiting beliefs. These are negative thoughts or assumptions about money that can obstruct wealth-building, such as the scarcity mindset, where individuals believe there's never enough money, or the notion that wealth is only attainable through luck or inheritance. Such beliefs can keep you from pursuing opportunities or making changes that could improve your financial situation. For example, if you believe you're simply not good with money, you might avoid learning about budgeting or investments, settling for less than what you could achieve financially. Recognizing these patterns allows you to challenge them and shift towards a mindset that supports financial growth and abundance (*Un-Limit Your Beliefs: Money Blocks and the Scarcity Mindset*, n.d.).

To effectively tackle these beliefs, it's crucial to identify personal stories that have contributed to them. Often, these narratives are rooted in childhood experiences, societal influences, or past financial struggles. By pinpointing the origin of these stories, you gain insight into why certain beliefs hold power over you. This awareness isn't just about looking back but about using this understanding to reshape your current perspective. For instance, someone who grew up hearing phrases like "money doesn't grow on trees" might internalize a belief in financial scarcity. By confronting these inherited narratives, you open the door to crafting a new story—one where financial abundance is possible and within reach.

Identifying these personal stories is key to overcoming limiting beliefs. Reflect on past experiences and narratives that have shaped your financial mindset. Understanding their roots can help in dismantling these mental barriers. Perhaps a belief formed because money was considered taboo in your family, or it was always linked to stress. Once you acknowledge these stories, you can begin the process of reframing them. This step is essential because it turns abstract awareness into concrete change, guiding you toward a more empowering narrative (Greer, 2022).

Reframing strategies come into play here. Techniques such as visualization or affirmations can be powerful tools in changing negative financial narratives into empowering stories. Visualization allows you to see yourself succeeding financially, providing a mental blueprint for real-world actions. Affirmations, on the other hand, reinforce positive beliefs daily, gradually shifting your mindset. Instead of telling yourself, "I'll never be able to save enough," try affirming, "I am capable of managing my finances effectively." This isn't merely about positive thinking but about building the confidence to take actionable steps toward financial goals. Empowering yourself with a healthier financial narrative makes it easier to pursue wealth-building initiatives with self-assurance.

In addition to personal work, seeking external support can be instrumental in overcoming these mental blocks. Surrounding yourself with like-minded individuals provides a community of encouragement and shared wisdom. Whether through financial literacy groups, mentorship, or networking, aligning yourself with people who understand and support your financial aspirations can create an environment conducive to growth. They not only provide valuable resources and motivation but also serve as reminders that your financial dreams are achievable. Engaging with others who have faced similar challenges can also provide practical insights and strategies that you may not have considered. Moreover, discussing financial goals and hurdles openly reduces the stigma and isolation surrounding money matters, fostering a supportive atmosphere where everyone can learn and grow together.

Creating a network of support is particularly vital for young professionals aiming to escape the paycheck-to-paycheck lifestyle. By engaging with financial advisors, joining professional networks, or even participating in online forums, they can gain fresh perspectives and strategies to enhance their financial situation. Middle-aged individuals planning for retirement can benefit from connecting with peers or mentors who have successfully navigated similar transitions, while entrepreneurs can explore mastermind groups focused on creating multiple streams of income. In each scenario, the key is to find those who not only inspire but also challenge you to think beyond your current limitations.

Developing a Growth Mindset

The journey to wealth accumulation is as much about cultivating the right mindset as it is about financial strategies. A critical component of this mindset is embracing adaptability and a willingness to learn, which can significantly impact one's financial success. This subpoint explores how these elements contribute to a thriving financial life.

The Power of Yet

One of the foundations for building wealth is understanding that growth is an ongoing process rather than a fixed outcome. This idea can be captured by embracing "the power of yet." This phrase signifies a belief in potential and skill development over time. Rather than seeing financial goals as distant achievements, viewing them through the lens of "not yet" allows individuals to focus on progress and learning. Adopting this mindset encourages an acceptance of imperfection while fostering resilience and determination. For example, if someone hasn't mastered investment strategies, acknowledging they haven't learned them "yet" opens doors for exploration and improvement. This approach not only motivates continuous effort but also reduces the fear of failure, paving the way for sustained personal and financial growth.

Continuous Learning

In the ever-evolving world of finance, continuous learning is paramount. Strategies for ongoing education encompass a variety of approaches that can benefit both young professionals and seasoned investors. Reading financial literature, attending workshops, and participating in online courses are effective ways to enhance financial literacy. Additionally, engaging with financial mentors or joining investment clubs can provide valuable insights and broaden understanding. These avenues offer opportunities to stay informed about market trends, economic shifts, and emerging investment vehicles, crucial for making informed decisions. The commitment to lifelong learning ensures that individuals remain proactive, adapting their financial strategies to align with current realities. Moreover, an informed investor is better equipped to navigate uncertainties and seize opportunities, fortifying their wealth-building pursuits.

Adaptability to Change

Adaptability is a cornerstone of successful wealth accumulation, especially given the unpredictable nature of economic landscapes. Flexibility in financial strategies allows individuals to pivot when necessary, safeguarding their assets and optimizing their portfolios. This flexibility might involve reassessing risk tolerance, diversifying investments, or adjusting savings plans in response to changing circumstances. For instance, during economic downturns, reallocating resources from volatile stocks to more stable bonds could mitigate losses. Similarly, being open to new technology-driven investment platforms, like robo-advisors or cryptocurrency, can expand one's financial repertoire. Embracing change instead of resisting it not only protects existing wealth but also positions individuals to capitalize on emerging trends and innovations. A flexible approach provides a buffer against market volatility while simultaneously unlocking potential avenues for growth.

Fostering Curiosity

Curiosity is an often-underestimated trait that can greatly enhance one's ability to accumulate wealth. By maintaining an open mind, individuals become receptive to diverse ideas and opportunities that may otherwise go unnoticed. Curiosity drives the urge to ask questions, explore different perspectives, and seek out novel experiences, all of which contribute to a richer understanding of financial dynamics. For entrepreneurs, this might mean exploring ancillary income streams or experimenting with unconventional business models. For investors, it could involve researching niche markets or alternative asset classes. Curiosity fosters innovation, encouraging creative problem-solving and strategic thinking, thereby nurturing an environment where wealth can flourish. Furthermore, curious individuals are more likely to embrace new learning opportunities, participate in financial discussions, and cultivate networks that facilitate resource sharing and collaboration.

Incorporating adaptability and a willingness to learn into one's financial mindset can profoundly shape the path to wealth accumulation. By leveraging the power of yet, committing to continuous education, embracing adaptability, and fostering curiosity, individuals position themselves for success in the complex world of finance. These elements not only enhance cognitive flexibility but also empower individuals to make informed choices, ultimately leading to a sustainable and prosperous financial future. It is through these mindset shifts that people can transcend traditional barriers, optimize their potential, and embark on a fulfilling journey toward financial independence. (https://www.facebook.com/theenlightenedcopywriter, 2024)

Importance of Perseverance and Discipline

In the pursuit of building wealth, persistence and self-control emerge as two critical pillars. These attributes are not merely personal virtues; they are essential components for anyone seeking financial success. Understanding how to integrate these traits into your financial journey can significantly enhance your ability to achieve and sustain wealth over the long term.

To begin with, setting long-term goals is foundational in cultivating a mindset conducive to wealth building. Financial success doesn't materialize overnight; it requires a clear vision and a strategic plan. Setting specific, measurable, achievable, relevant, and time-bound (SMART) goals provides a roadmap that keeps you aligned and focused. For instance, instead of a vague intention like "get rich," a concrete goal might be "save $50,000 for a down payment on a house in five years." This clarity not only motivates but also sets a benchmark against which progress can be measured, helping maintain momentum even when challenges arise.

Creating consistent habits is another crucial aspect. Wealth building is as much about daily decisions as it is about long-term strategy. By developing disciplined routines that align with your financial goals, you set yourself up for sustained success. Consider creating a habit of regular savings or investing a fixed percentage of your income each month. Such practices, when done consistently over time, accumulate into significant financial growth. As noted by experts, our brains are wired to form habits through repetition, thus making consistent actions almost automatic over time (Gleeson, 2020). This automatization allows individuals to avoid the pitfalls of procrastination and impulsive spending, ensuring that their financial endeavors remain on track.

Accountability practices also play an indispensable role in maintaining persistence and self-control. Utilizing tools like budgeting apps or spreadsheets can provide a visual track of your financial health, illuminating areas of improvement and highlighting successes. Beyond tools, becoming part of a community or accountability group can offer support and encouragement. Sharing your goals with a partner or group can provide a sense of responsibility and external motivation. These groups can offer advice, share experiences, and keep you accountable to your commitments, thereby fostering an environment that supports your financial objectives.

Celebrating discipline is equally important in this journey. Recognizing and rewarding oneself for maintaining consistent and disciplined efforts can reinforce positive behavior and motivate continued perseverance. Celebrations need not be extravagant; a small reward for reaching a milestone can suffice. Acknowledging achievements helps combat the fatigue that can accompany long-term financial plans. It provides a psychological boost and reinforces the belief that you are on the right path, encouraging persistence despite the inevitable obstacles that may arise.

These principles—setting long-term goals, creating consistent habits, using accountability practices, and celebrating discipline—should be integrated into everyday life. For young professionals eager to escape the paycheck-to-paycheck cycle, establishing such structures early can have compounding benefits over time. Middle-aged individuals planning for retirement will find that these strategies help ensure their investments provide for a comfortable future. Entrepreneurs looking to diversify income streams can rely on these same tactics to manage multiple financial ventures effectively.

Moreover, embracing the occasional setbacks in wealth-building as opportunities for growth is crucial. This mindset shift isn't just about resilience; it's about learning from mistakes to refine your approach continuously. For example, if an investment doesn't yield expected returns, instead of viewing it as a failure, examine what went wrong, adjust your strategy, and persist with renewed insight. This process of learning and adjustment is vital for long-term success in any financial endeavor.

Embracing Failure as Learning

In the journey of wealth accumulation, reframing setbacks as opportunities for growth is crucial. This mindset shift enables individuals to view financial missteps not as failures, but as valuable lessons that inform future decisions. The ability to extract insights from each setback and apply them proactively transforms potential roadblocks into stepping stones.

Understanding that every financial misstep provides valuable lessons is central to this perspective. Consider the stories of Henry Ford and Thomas Edison—both faced considerable failures, yet these setbacks were integral to their ultimate success. As an aspiring wealth builder, adopting a similar approach encourages viewing errors not with regret, but as educational moments that refine strategy and decision-making skills (Webster, 2024).

Celebrating small wins along the financial journey can build confidence and set the stage for facing larger challenges. Achieving minor goals, such as saving a specific amount or successfully cutting unnecessary expenses, reinforces positive behavior and boosts morale. This incremental progress not only enhances self-assurance but also cultivates resilience, making it easier to handle more substantial financial hurdles. Steve Jobs's career exemplifies this: his return to Apple after years spent building other ventures underscored how leveraging small victories contributes to broader successes (Webster, 2024).

Persistence through adversity remains a key factor in long-term financial goal achievement. Resilience enables individuals to maintain focus despite difficulties, reinforcing their commitment to objectives. Overcoming financial obstacles strengthens one's discipline and fosters adaptability—a skillset crucial for sustained development. The story of entrepreneurs who have navigated multiple failures illustrates that persistent effort, combined with the willingness to learn from each experience, ultimately leads to success (Shakir, 2024).

Sharing experiences with others further enriches the journey, reducing feelings of isolation while providing fresh insights into overcoming challenges. Engaging with peers, mentors, and advisors can offer diverse perspectives and invaluable guidance. These interactions serve not only as emotional support but also expand one's understanding of various strategies to manage wealth effectively. Networking with financial literacy groups can foster accountability and prompt individuals to stay committed to their financial goals. Moreover, finding mentors who provide personalized feedback helps navigate complex choices, offering a pathway through uncharted financial landscapes (Webster, 2024).

Indeed, setbacks are inevitable, but they need not be detrimental. Engaging in honest reflection on the causes behind each setback allows for a deeper comprehension of personal and systemic shortcomings. By identifying these root causes, one can implement changes to prevent recurrence and enhance overall decision-making processes. This proactive approach reflects a commitment to continuous improvement and positions setbacks as integral components of the learning process.

Additionally, developing realistic milestones within larger financial ambitions helps individuals break down overwhelming goals into achievable steps. This strategy mitigates the fear of failure by emphasizing progress rather than perfection, leading to steady advancement toward financial stability. Coupled with celebrating small victories, setting attainable targets has the potential to transform daunting financial endeavors into rewarding journeys (Shakir, 2024).

The narratives of business icons like Ford and Edison further highlight the importance of resilience and strategic adaptation over time. For young professionals seeking to escape the cycle of living paycheck-to-paycheck, cultivating these traits is essential. Similarly, middle-aged individuals planning for retirement can benefit by applying these principles to ensure their savings grow sustainably, without succumbing to common pitfalls. Entrepreneurs, meanwhile, can draw from this wisdom to diversify income streams and bolster their financial portfolios (Webster, 2024; Shakir, 2024).

Insights and Implications

In this chapter, we've explored the critical components of developing a mindset that paves the way for financial success. Recognizing and challenging limiting beliefs is key to unlocking your potential. These mental barriers often stem from childhood narratives or societal influences that convince us financial abundance is unattainable. By identifying these deeply rooted stories, you gain the power to reshape your perspective and adopt beliefs that support growth. We also discussed strategies such as visualization and affirmations to reframe negative thoughts into positive ones. This transformation empowers you to approach wealth-building with confidence and clarity.

Moreover, surrounding yourself with a supportive community enhances this journey. Engaging with like-minded individuals—whether through financial literacy groups, mentorship, or networking—provides motivation and valuable insights. Such connections can inspire new strategies and reinforce your commitment to creating a prosperous financial future. For young professionals, this means stepping out of the paycheck-to-paycheck cycle; middle-aged individuals can secure their retirement plans, while entrepreneurs can explore diverse income streams. Embracing adaptability and continuous learning equips you with the tools needed to navigate the complexities of finance, ultimately leading to a sustainable and thriving financial life.

Reference List

Burns, S. (2024, October 8). *Poor People Rules* . New Trader U. https://www.newtraderu.com/2024/10/08/5-money-lessons-that-separate-the-rich-from-the-poor-based-on-self-discipline-and-psychology/

Greer, D. A. (2022, October 24). *15 Top Money Blocks Limiting Your Abundance* . Ashlee Greer. https://www.ashleegreer.com/top-money-blocks-limiting-your-abundance/

Gleeson, B. (2020, August 25). *8 Powerful Ways To Cultivate Extreme Self-Discipline* . Forbes. https://www.forbes.com/sites/brentgleeson/2020/08/25/8-powerful-ways-to-cultivate-extreme-self-discipline/

Olivier, C. (2024, March 7). *Accumulating Wealth vs. Managing Wealth: Navigating the Dual Realities of Financial Success* . RegInsights. https://www.regenesys.net/reginsights/accumulating-wealth-vs-managing-wealth-navigating-the-dual-realities-of-financial-success

Shakir, A. (2024, November 29). *How to Handle Business Setbacks and Turn Them Into Opportunities* : Medium. https://medium.com/@shakir.489933/how-to-handle-business-setbacks-and-turn-them-into-opportunities-df01b5771897

Un-Limit Your Beliefs: Money Blocks and the Scarcity Mindset . (n.d.). Www.ipeccoaching.com. https://www.ipeccoaching.com/blog/money-blocks-and-the-scarcity-mindset/

Webster, J. (2024, May 23). *Turning Setbacks into Success: Entrepreneur Stories* . ROK Financial. https://www.rok.biz/blog/from-failure-to-fortune-how-entrepreneurs-turn-setbacks-into-stepping-stones/

https://www.facebook.com/theenlightenedcopywriter. (2024, October 12). *Why Continuous Learning Impacts Wealth Creation* . Millionaire Mindset Roadmap. https://millionairemindsetroadmap.com/why-continuous-learning-impacts-wealth-creation/

Chapter 11

Common Mistakes and How to Avoid Them

Avoiding common financial mistakes is essential for building a secure economic future. Recognizing the traps and challenges that can undermine financial stability enables individuals to make informed decisions, safeguarding their investments and assets. This chapter delves into the various pitfalls that often trip up young professionals, middle-aged individuals planning for retirement, and entrepreneurs looking to expand their income streams. The financial landscape is rife with opportunities, but it is equally filled with potential missteps that can derail even the most prudent plans. Understanding these risks and learning how to navigate them is crucial for anyone aiming to maintain or enhance their financial standing.

Throughout the chapter, readers will explore detailed insights on how to identify misleading investment opportunities and avoid over-leverage. The discussion extends to real-world examples illustrating the consequences of excessive risk-taking and the importance of maintaining a balanced approach. It also highlights strategies for effective debt management, ensuring that borrowing does not lead to broader financial difficulties. By examining past financial errors, the chapter provides valuable lessons on how to recognize repeating patterns and implement corrective measures. Personal anecdotes and expert advice offer a practical framework for avoiding common mistakes, empowering readers with the knowledge to avoid financial pitfalls and set themselves on a path to long-term economic health.

Recognizing Misleading Investment Opportunities

In today's dynamic financial landscape, spotting and avoiding deceptive investments is a critical skill for anyone seeking to safeguard their economic future. Many investors, whether young professionals striving for financial independence, middle-aged individuals planning retirement, or entrepreneurs expanding their income streams, can fall prey to too-good-to-be-true investment opportunities. Recognizing the warning signs of these traps is essential for securing one's finances.

Misleading promises of high returns are often the first indicator of a potential scam. The allure of substantial, guaranteed profits with minimal effort can be enticing, but these claims often conceal high levels of risk or out-and-out fraud. A prudent investor understands that all investments carry some level of risk; therefore, any assertion of risk-free high returns should immediately signal caution. It is vital to remember that legitimate investments will not offer unrealistic gains without commensurate risk.

Adding to this, high-pressure sales tactics present another red flag. Scammers frequently employ these methods to push individuals into rash decisions, creating an artificial sense of urgency or claiming the need to act quickly before others seize the opportunity. These tactics are designed to prevent thorough research and reflection. An authentic investment opportunity allows for careful consideration and due diligence. Thus, feeling rushed or cornered into making swift investment decisions without adequate information should trigger skepticism.

To combat the pitfalls of deceptive investments, leveraging multiple sources for validation is indispensable. Cross-referencing details across different independent resources helps construct a fuller and more accurate picture of the offering in question. This might include checking the credentials of those promoting the investment, verifying the company's history through online reviews or regulatory database checks, and seeking out professional critiques or analyses. Instead of relying on one source, employing several can provide a buffer against misleading presentations, as inconsistencies might emerge that warrant further investigation.

Researching the investment comprehensively prior to engagement is not merely advisable; it is crucial. Begin with a deep dive into the history and reputation of the person or organization proposing the deal. Look closely at their professional record, including past dealings and any legal entanglements that might have arisen. Additionally, evaluating their qualifications can give insight into their expertise and reliability. Always seek written documentation that covers all aspects of the proposed investment.

Consulting with advisors who hold a fiduciary duty is another powerful strategy to avoid falling victim to deceitful schemes. Advisors with this duty are legally obligated to act in your best interest rather than their own or their firm's, thus prioritizing your financial wellbeing above personal gain. Engaging with such professionals ensures advice grounded in truth and protection rather than ulterior motives. Importantly, consulting an advisor offers an informed second opinion, which is critical when weighing the merits and risks of a new investment proposition.

Seeking professional advice provides an external perspective that can shed light on intricate financial nuances that may be overlooked. Pursue guidance from financial experts who can demystify complex details and validate the legitimacy of the potential venture. They serve as a safeguard against manipulation and emphasize the importance of clear, informed decision-making. Furthermore, working with trusted advisors means you gain access to their network and experience, serving as a rich resource for knowledge and support.

Through examining real-world scenarios where fraudulent activities have deceived unsuspecting investors, we learn valuable lessons. Many scams involve elaborate narratives designed to persuade the unwary. For instance, Ponzi schemes notoriously captivate by paying returns to earlier investors using the capital from newer ones, only surviving until the inflow of money halts. Such cases underscore the necessity of vigilance and skepticism, reinforcing the idea that investigating every facet of an investment is imperative.

Lastly, personal experience and shared stories from peers can offer profound insights. Learning from the missteps of those who came before can foster a cautious approach in evaluating opportunities. Whether through informal discussions or structured networking events, knowledge exchange helps raise awareness about prevalent deceitful practices.

Avoiding Over-Leverage and Excessive Risk

Leverage is often seen as a powerful tool in the world of finance. By borrowing funds, individuals and businesses can potentially amplify their returns on investment. However, leverage is a double-edged sword that magnifies losses as well as gains. Consider the scenario of purchasing a property using borrowed money. If the property's value increases, the returns are substantial compared to the initial equity input. Conversely, if the market turns and the property value decreases, the losses incurred could be devastating, especially if they exceed the original investment amount.

A critical aspect of maintaining financial stability involves understanding personal risk tolerance. Each individual's comfort with risk varies, influenced by factors such as financial goals, time horizon, and emotional resilience. For instance, a young professional with decades until retirement might tolerate higher risks for greater potential rewards than someone nearing retirement age who may prefer security over volatility. Establishing a clear sense of one's risk tolerance is crucial. It allows for crafting an investment strategy tailored to one's unique circumstances, ensuring decisions made during fluctuating markets align with long-term objectives.

Understanding risk tolerance is not just about theoretical knowledge; practical application demands regular reassessment of investments against life changes and shifting economic landscapes. Including a guideline on assessing and adjusting this risk tolerance periodically ensures better alignment with evolving personal and market conditions.

Diversity within an investment portfolio plays an indispensable role in safeguarding against market volatility. A well-diversified portfolio spreads risk across various asset classes—such as stocks, bonds, real estate, and more—thus reducing exposure to any single economic sector's downturn. This approach increases resilience, as the decline in one area can be offset by stability or growth in another. Diversification serves as a buffer in uncertain times, acting as a cornerstone for financial stability. Young professionals, in particular, should be encouraged to explore multiple investment vehicles early on, allowing compounding to work to their advantage over time.

Middle-aged individuals planning for retirement also benefit significantly from portfolio diversification. At this stage, incorporating low-risk investments alongside more aggressive ones helps protect accumulated wealth while providing opportunities for growth. Entrepreneurship and creating passive income streams further enhance financial security, allowing individuals to explore beyond their primary business interests responsibly.

Guidance on diversification includes considering investment options and balancing them based on one's life stage and financial goals, helping readers create a robust investment strategy that stays aligned with their future needs.

Historical financial downturns offer valuable lessons on the importance of prudence and preparation. The 2008 global financial crisis serves as a stark reminder of how excessive leveraging led to widespread economic turmoil. Over-leveraged institutions found themselves unable to meet financial obligations, resulting in severe repercussions across global markets. The aftermath demonstrated the necessity for thorough risk assessment and strategic foresight. Individuals and businesses must heed these lessons and incorporate strategies that account for potential economic downturns.

This involves maintaining emergency funds, regularly reviewing and adjusting leverage levels, and monitoring economic indicators to anticipate shifts that may impact financial well-being. Continuous education and awareness of historical contexts empower individuals to make informed decisions, avoiding past mistakes. The Reflective analysis on previous downturns provides insight into human behavior during crises, emphasizing rational decision-making in situations prone to panic and uncertainty.

Effective debt management is another vital component in achieving financial stability. While some level of debt is commonplace and even beneficial under certain circumstances, uncontrolled accumulation leads to financial strain. Managing debt proactively involves creating a comprehensive payment plan, prioritizing high-interest debts to minimize overall costs. Tools like budget tracking applications or consultation with financial advisors can aid in developing a realistic and manageable repayment strategy.

Moreover, individuals should remain vigilant about their credit scores, as these directly influence borrowing terms and interest rates. Maintaining a healthy credit profile through timely payments and responsible borrowing practices enables access to favorable financial products, enhancing purchasing power and reducing financial stress. Entrepreneurs, in particular, need to balance leveraging their businesses for growth with maintaining sustainable debt levels to foster long-term success.

By integrating effective debt management practices, cultivating a diverse investment portfolio, and acknowledging personal risk tolerance, individuals across varying life stages fortify themselves against common financial pitfalls. These efforts collectively promote financial resilience, equipping individuals with the tools necessary to build secure futures for themselves and generations to follow.

Learning from Past Financial Mistakes

Avoiding common financial errors requires a proactive approach. Recognizing these mistakes is the first vital step towards devising strategies that prevent them from occurring in the future. Many times, financial mishaps result from a lack of awareness or understanding, which underscores the significance of educating oneself about foundational financial principles.

One of the most prevalent mistakes is not having a structured spending plan. As highlighted by experts at the University of Nebraska-Lincoln, creating a budget allows individuals to visualize their income and expenses, helping them maintain financial balance (*6 Common Money Management Mistakes College Students Make | Announce | University of Nebraska-Lincoln*, 2012). By comparing expenditures with earnings, it becomes clearer where adjustments are necessary to ensure one is living within their means. This simple yet powerful tool can help avoid overspending, a common pitfall for many, especially young professionals starting their careers.

Case studies serve as compelling narratives, showcasing how recovery from financial blunders is possible and highlighting resilience and growth. For instance, consider the anecdote of a young entrepreneur who faced substantial debt due to over-reliance on credit cards. Initially using credit to cover gaps, they soon found themselves buried under high-interest payments that consumed a significant portion of their monthly earnings. By acknowledging this mistake and crafting a meticulous repayment strategy, they not only managed to clear their debt but also learned essential budgeting skills. This transformative journey is illustrative of how identifying an error can lead to profound personal and financial growth.

Continuous education in financial literacy is another cornerstone of avoiding financial pitfalls. Knowledge empowers individuals to make informed decisions, whether about everyday expenditures or more complex investment opportunities. According to Metro Community, neglecting financial planning can severely hinder long-term savings efforts (Metro Community, 2022). Educating oneself about different budgeting methods, such as the 50/30/20 rule, which allocates 50% for needs, 30% for wants, and 20% for savings and investments, provides a framework for effective financial management. Financial literacy courses, workshops, and online resources can further enhance understanding, enabling individuals to navigate financial challenges with greater efficacy.

Developing a mistake-correction plan is crucial to mitigate the impact of financial errors when they

Personal Finance Strategies

occur. Recognizing a misstep promptly can curtail its negative consequences. A well-crafted plan should include steps like reassessing one's current financial standing, identifying areas of leakage, and setting realistic goals for recovery. It might involve trimming discretionary spending, renegotiating terms with creditors, or even seeking professional financial advice to devise a tailored strategy. Just as businesses execute risk management plans, individuals can employ similar tactics to safeguard their financial health.

Moreover, surrounding oneself with a supportive network can make a significant difference. Peer pressure and societal expectations often drive individuals to make poor financial choices. Encouraging open dialogues about money among friends, family, and mentors can foster an environment where it's safe to discuss financial concerns without judgment. This social support can act as a buffer against impulsive decisions that could derail financial progress.

Leveraging technology can also be a game-changer in managing personal finances. Numerous apps offer features like expense tracking, budget creation, and goal setting. Platforms such as Mint provide users with a comprehensive view of their financial activities, enabling them to spot anomalies early and adjust accordingly. These digital tools add a layer of convenience and accessibility, crucial for those striving to escape the paycheck-to-paycheck cycle.

It's also important to remember that financial errors don't define one's entire financial journey. Mistakes are stepping stones to improvement if approached constructively. Reflecting on what went wrong, why it happened, and how it can be avoided in the future transforms a setback into a learning opportunity. Embracing a mindset of continuous improvement and adaptability prepares individuals for unexpected challenges.

When planning for retirement, middle-aged individuals must be particularly cautious of financial pitfalls. As they transition from active income-generating years to relying on accumulated wealth, understanding common errors like underestimating longevity or healthcare costs becomes paramount. Incorporating regular financial reviews can ensure their retirement strategies remain aligned with changing circumstances and life goals.

Entrepreneurs, too, need to be vigilant. The allure of expanding business operations or diversifying income streams can sometimes overshadow prudent financial practices. Developing a robust mistake-correction plan enables them to pivot swiftly in response to financial setbacks, preserving both their ventures and personal finances.

Educating on Financial Safety Measures

In today's complex financial landscape, understanding the intricacies of financial instruments can significantly reduce vulnerability to scams. For young professionals eager to leave behind a paycheck-to-paycheck existence, knowledge about different financial tools—from stocks and bonds to mutual funds and retirement accounts—is invaluable. A solid grasp of these financial avenues ensures they can make informed decisions that align with their specific goals. Understanding these tools not only helps in recognizing legitimate opportunities but also aids in spotting potential frauds which often exploit ignorance around financial matters. As noted by Schwab (2021), setting clear financial goals is key for anyone trying to plan effectively, and doing so requires an understanding of the available financial instruments.

Similarly, middle-aged individuals planning for retirement must navigate various options to maximize their savings and investments. By learning about annuities, pensions, and other retirement-specific products, they can safeguard their financial future. This level of comprehension demystifies the decision-making process and empowers them to protect their assets from deceitful schemes that might otherwise deplete their retirement nest egg.

Seeking expert advice is another vital pillar in strengthening financial protection plans. Financial planners, certified financial advisors, or even reputable robo-advisors offer tailored strategies based on individual circumstances. For entrepreneurs looking to diversify their income streams, professional guidance helps evaluate risk factors and growth potential accurately. An advisor's expertise offers invaluable insights into optimizing tax strategies, identifying profitable ventures, and ensuring compliance with regulatory standards, ultimately fortifying one's overall financial health. It's crucial to remember, as Manning (2023) highlighted, that a well-crafted financial plan should be revisited regularly, especially when new income opportunities arise.

Monitoring financial progress is essential for identifying and rectifying emerging issues before they escalate into significant problems. Regular assessment of one's financial standing—through detailed tracking of income, expenses, debts, and investments—paves the way for timely corrections. Young professionals, through diligent monitoring, can understand their spending patterns, cut unnecessary expenditures, and channel savings toward more lucrative investment opportunities. Entrepreneurs benefit too, as consistent evaluation allows them to adapt to market changes swiftly and maintain a steady flow of revenue across multiple income streams.

For those approaching retirement, regular checks on retirement account balances, projected social security benefits, and living expense estimates ensure their retirement plans remain viable and aligned with life expectancy increases. This practice not only prevents potential shortfalls but also provides peace of mind that can only come from being prepared.

Building a robust safety net is another critical strategy in preparing for unforeseen economic challenges. Having an emergency fund, as advised by Yahoo! Finance, is a fundamental component of any secure financial plan. Whether it's job loss, unexpected medical expenses, or economic recession, a well-stocked emergency fund acts as a financial cushion. Saving three to six months' worth of living expenses is recommended, providing a buffer against life's unpredictable events.

For entrepreneurs, establishing an emergency reserve can mean the difference between sustaining the business during downturns or facing closure. It ensures that operations continue smoothly without compromising employee salaries or quality of service. Similarly, for individuals nearing retirement, having additional funds set aside beyond traditional retirement savings accounts can cover sudden inflation hikes or healthcare needs.

Implementing these strategies involves understanding that every financial journey is unique, requiring a personalized approach to planning. Nonetheless, the foundational principles of awareness, expert consultation, continuous monitoring, and contingency preparations are universally applicable. These components collectively nurture a secure financial future, allowing individuals to thrive economically regardless of their life stage or professional aspirations.

Final Thoughts

In this chapter, we have explored the various strategies to identify and prevent common financial pitfalls that can impact individuals across different life stages. For young professionals eager to gain financial independence, recognizing misleading investment opportunities and understanding personal risk tolerance are critical skills for building a secure future. By emphasizing the importance of due diligence and leveraging expert advice, we outlined ways to navigate the complexities of investments and safeguarding one's finances. For middle-aged individuals planning for retirement, the focus was on evaluating and diversifying their portfolios to ensure a steady stream of income, considering their unique financial needs. Meanwhile, entrepreneurs were guided on establishing additional income streams while balancing leverage with sustainable debt management to promote long-term success.

Throughout the chapter, key lessons from past financial mistakes were highlighted, illustrating how personal experiences and professional advice play pivotal roles in informed decision-making. Maintaining a well-rounded approach—spanning from continuous education in financial literacy to effective debt management and portfolio diversification—serves as a formidable shield against potential economic downturns. Additionally, the integration of technology in financial planning was discussed, offering practical tools that empower individuals to monitor and adjust their financial strategies proactively. As each audience tailors these insights to their own circumstances, the journey towards financial resilience becomes clearer, enabling them to secure a future aligned with their aspirations and goals.

Reference List

3. Leverage in the Financial Sector . (n.d.). Www.federalreserve.gov. https://www.federalreserve.gov/publications/2023-may-financial-stability-report-leverage.htm

6 Common Money Management Mistakes College Students Make | Announce | University of Nebraska-Lincoln . (2012, August 14). Newsroom.unl.edu. https://newsroom.unl.edu/announce/parentnews/1426/8291

Investment Fraud Lawyers. (2024, March 12). *Recognizing And Avoiding Investment Fraud: 10 Tips For Investors* . Investment Fraud Lawyers. https://investmentfraudlawyers.com/recognizing-

and-avoiding-investment-fraud-10-tips-for-investors/

Leveraged Lending: Evolution, Growth and Heightened Risk | FDIC . (2024). Fdic.gov. https://www.fdic.gov/bank-examinations/leveraged-lending-evolution-growth-and-heightened-risk

Metro Community. (2022, November 2). *7 Common Financial Mistakes - Metro Community Development* . Metro Community Development. https://metrocommunitydevelopment.com/7-common-financial-mistakes/

Manning, L. (2023, November 30). *Understanding Financial Plans* . Investopedia. https://www.investopedia.com/terms/f/financial_plan.asp

Securities Fraud Defense Strategies for Denver Clients – Masterson Hall . (2024). Mastersonhall.com. https://www.mastersonhall.com/securities-fraud-defense-strategies-for-denver-clients/

Schwab, C. (2021). *8 Components of a Good Financial Plan* . Schwab Brokerage. https://www.schwab.com/financial-planning-collection/8-components-of-good-financial-plan

Chapter 12

Conclusion: Your Path to a Carefree Lifestyle

Achieving a carefree lifestyle through financial freedom is a journey filled with unique challenges and rewards. As we conclude this exploration, it's vital to understand that the pursuit of economic independence doesn't necessarily follow a single, linear path. Instead, it comprises a diverse array of strategies and choices that cater to individual circumstances and goals. Whether you're a young professional eager to break free from living paycheck to paycheck, a middle-aged adult preparing for retirement, or an entrepreneur expanding your income streams, the road to financial freedom requires thoughtful planning and consistent action. Each step taken represents a building block in crafting a personalized blueprint toward a more secure and liberated future.

This chapter delves into a comprehensive review of the key strategies essential for navigating your path toward financial autonomy. From the fundamentals of budgeting and managing debt to the intricacies of investing and diversifying income sources, you'll be equipped with the tools necessary to make informed financial decisions. By examining real-life stories of individuals who have successfully applied these strategies, this chapter aims to inspire and motivate you to take concrete steps in your own life. Valuable insights on creating personalized action plans and the significance of continuous learning will also be highlighted. Embrace the guidance offered here, and empower yourself to transform theoretical knowledge into practical application, ultimately setting the stage for a lifetime of financial well-being.

Recap Key Strategies and Insights

As we wrap up our exploration of financial freedom, it's essential to revisit the strategies that have been discussed throughout this book, reinforcing how they can effectively be applied. The journey towards financial independence is not a one-size-fits-all solution but rather a combination of tailored approaches that require active participation and adaptability for long-term stability.

First, let's recapture the key strategies that have been highlighted. Achieving financial freedom often begins with budgeting, where understanding your income and expenses allows you to make informed decisions. It's crucial to set realistic savings goals, ensuring you're consistently putting aside funds for emergencies and future investments. Moreover, managing debt wisely through structured repayment plans can prevent interest from eroding your savings.

Investing plays a significant role in building wealth. Diversifying your portfolio across different asset classes—such as stocks, bonds, and real estate—mitigates risks while maximizing growth potential. These financial tools offer compounding benefits over time, which strengthens financial resilience. Establishing multiple streams of income, whether through side businesses or passive investment opportunities, can further bolster financial security.

Combining these strategies requires adopting a mindset geared toward sustained success. For instance, merging disciplined budgeting with strategic investments amplifies benefits. This approach is akin to creating a financial ecosystem where each component supports the other, resulting in robust financial health.

However, it's equally important to be aware of potential missteps along the way. Common pitfalls include neglecting to update savings and investment goals as circumstances change or failing to allocate enough for contingencies. Vigilance in tracking financial progress helps avoid such errors. Regular reviews of your financial plan ensure accountability and provide an opportunity to adjust to shifting priorities or market conditions.

The stories of those who have successfully achieved financial freedom serve as both inspiration and proof of what is possible. Consider Jane, who at 35 found herself deep in credit card debt with no savings. Through a diligent application of budgeting techniques and targeted debt reduction, she managed to pay off her debts within three years. Her story demonstrates the power of commitment and the effectiveness of small, consistent steps toward financial autonomy.

Similarly, Michael, an entrepreneur, diversified his income sources by investing in rental properties alongside his primary business. By sticking to his plan and welcoming the challenge of market fluctuations, he's now enjoying a comfortable retirement ahead of schedule. Such stories highlight the transformative impact of implementing learned strategies effectively and adapting them to one's personal circumstances.

To encourage readers to take action, it's crucial to emphasize the importance of revisiting their notes and applying these concepts regularly. Financial education is an ongoing process. Just as the market evolves, so too should our strategies and understanding. Committing to continuous learning equips you with the knowledge needed to remain agile and innovative in your financial pursuits.

Recognize that every step taken towards financial freedom is worthwhile. It's about building habits that support wise spending, saving, and investing decisions throughout life. A proactive approach to tracing financial paths ensures they lead toward independence, free from the anxieties associated with economic instability.

Creating a Personalized Action Plan

Crafting an actionable and individualized plan for financial freedom requires setting clear, strategic goals that acknowledge personal circumstances. A pivotal aspect of this journey is defining SMART goals—Specific, Measurable, Achievable, Relevant, and Time-bound objectives tailored to each individual's financial vision. Establishing these goals offers a foundation upon which a personalized path to financial independence can be built. By concretely identifying what financial freedom looks like for you, it's possible to align your aspirations with realistic milestones that cater to your lifestyle and priorities. This approach not only ensures clarity but also enhances motivation towards achieving long-term success (Setting SMART Financial Goals,

2024; SMART Goals for Your Financial Plan, 2022).

Embarking on the pathway to financial freedom begins with an honest financial review. Understanding where you stand financially provides a comprehensive view of your current strengths and weaknesses. This process involves evaluating your income, expenses, debts, savings, and investments, offering a baseline from which to work. Reflect on how much money you have coming in versus going out, noting any discrepancies or areas of concern. It's equally important to consider both short-term and long-term financial obligations as part of this assessment. This introspective journey allows you to identify patterns, opportunities for improvement, and potential risks that need addressing. Solving existing issues and planning proactively based on these insights can prevent obstacles from derailing your progress in the future.

Once you've thoroughly assessed your financial landscape, personalizing investment and income strategies is crucial. This step involves tailoring your approach to align with your goals while remaining adaptable to change. Flexibility is key in adapting to market fluctuations, life transitions, and evolving economic conditions. One effective strategy is diversifying income streams—such as exploring freelance work, side businesses, or passive income avenues—which can provide a safety net against uncertainty and enhance your financial stability. Diversification not only spreads risk but also capitalizes on different sectors' growth, increasing your wealth-building potential. Moreover, keeping abreast of financial trends and consulting experts when needed can help you adjust your strategies effectively, ensuring they remain relevant and aligned with your overarching objectives.

Progress tracking and milestone setting serve as the motivational fuel for realizing financial goals. Regularly monitoring your progress helps you stay on track, allowing for timely adjustments if necessary. Implementing tools such as budgeting apps or spreadsheets can simplify this process, providing a clear overview of your finances at any given moment. Celebrating milestones, whether big or small, reinforces commitment and increases morale along your financial journey. These celebrations remind you of your accomplishments and encourage you to keep striving toward your larger objectives. Whether it's paying off a significant portion of debt, reaching a savings target, or surpassing an investment goal, taking time to acknowledge these victories nurtures a positive mindset and sustained motivation throughout your financial journey.

Encouragement to Pursue Financial Independence

Embarking on the journey to financial independence is akin to climbing a mountain: it requires endurance, planning, and continuous motivation. One of the most crucial aspects of this endeavor is the recognition and celebration of small victories. Each milestone, no matter how minor it may seem at the time, brings you closer to your ultimate goal of financial freedom. By celebrating these achievements, you maintain a sense of motivation and reinforce the progress you've made along your wealth journey.

For many, the road to financial independence can be long and filled with challenges. Acknowledging your successes, such as paying off a credit card or reaching a savings goal, provides tangible evidence that your efforts are paying off. These celebrations serve not only as motivational boosts but also as reminders of what you can accomplish when you put your mind to it. This practice strengthens your resolve, helping you stay committed to your larger financial goals.

Equally important in your quest for financial independence is connecting with like-minded communities. Surrounding yourself with individuals who share similar goals and ambitions can be incredibly inspiring and invaluable. By participating in these communities, you have the opportunity to share your experiences, learn from others, and explore growth opportunities together. This mutual support fosters an environment where members inspire each other, pushing themselves toward greater achievements.

Imagine being part of a group where members routinely share stories of their hardships and triumphs. As you listen to others' journeys—how they tackled student loans or successfully invested in the stock market—you gain insight and strategies that might apply to your situation. More importantly, witnessing others achieve their goals reinforces the notion that financial independence is attainable, bolstering your own determination.

As financial landscapes continuously evolve, staying informed about current trends and strategies becomes paramount. Continuous learning ensures that you remain adaptable and capable of navigating changes effectively. In an era defined by rapid technological advancements and economic shifts, understanding innovative financial strategies can mean the difference between stagnation and progress.

Attending webinars, enrolling in courses, or even reading up-to-date books and articles keeps your knowledge fresh. For instance, exploring new investment opportunities, such as cryptocurrency or sustainable funds, allows you to diversify your portfolio and potentially increase your wealth. By remaining informed and flexible, you place yourself in a favorable position to capitalize on evolving trends, thereby enhancing your ability to secure financial freedom.

Despite the many tools and resources available, cultivating a resilient financial mindset remains at the heart of any successful wealth-building journey. This mindset is characterized by positive thinking, persistence, and unwavering commitment to your financial ambitions. It means developing the belief that financial setbacks are not failures but rather learning experiences. This outlook transforms obstacles into stepping stones, pushing you forward rather than dragging you down.

Consider the power of positive affirmations and perseverance when faced with economic downturns or personal financial mishaps. Instead of succumbing to negativity, remind yourself of past successes and the possibilities that lie ahead. Persistence is the glue that holds your financial strategy together, ensuring you remain focused on your long-term objectives despite short-term challenges.

An often overlooked but vital component of achieving financial independence is accountability. It's essential not only to commit to your plan but also to hold yourself accountable throughout the journey. Consider keeping journals or using apps to track your expenses and savings targets. Similarly, partnering with someone—a mentor or friend—who can check in on your progress adds an extra layer of responsibility.

Moreover, educating yourself about potential missteps that could derail your financial journey is critical. Understanding common pitfalls, such as overspending or inadequate emergency savings, prepares you to navigate around them effectively. Maintaining vigilance over your spending habits and investments ensures that you are proactively managing your wealth-building strategies (Batsters & Batsters, 2024).

Ultimately, the path to financial independence demands dedication, strategy, and resilience. Celebrating small victories, engaging with supportive communities, embracing continuous learning, and cultivating a robust financial mindset are all essential steps in this process. Together, these components create a roadmap that guides you toward a future free from financial stress—a future where you have the freedom to pursue life on your terms.

Taking Confident Steps Forward

To genuinely inspire readers to embark on their journey towards financial freedom, it's crucial to embrace an approach that is both proactive and goal-oriented. By doing so, individuals can take charge of their financial futures with the confidence needed to navigate the complexities that lie ahead. This mindset involves setting clear and achievable goals, allowing for a roadmap that guides every financial decision made along the way. A proactive approach means actively seeking opportunities to improve one's financial situation rather than waiting for change to happen passively. Goal orientation ensures that there is always a destination in sight, providing motivation and direction.

Informed decision-making plays a significant role in this process. Leveraging insights from proven strategies presented throughout the book, readers can make decisions grounded in knowledge and understanding. For instance, incorporating lessons from financial analysis enables accurate assessments of personal or business finances, contributing to smarter allocation of resources and identification of potential investment opportunities (GAVIN, 2020). Such informed choices are imperative in avoiding common pitfalls and ensuring that every step taken is aligned with broader financial objectives.

As readers internalize these principles, the transition from theoretical knowledge to practical application becomes essential. The book not only equips individuals with strategies but also empowers them to implement these techniques in real-world scenarios. Whether it's creating effective budgets, managing debts wisely, or exploring diverse income streams, these methodologies are designed to be adaptable and relevant to various stages of life. The ability to apply learned skills in navigating everyday financial challenges and significant life events is what transforms knowledge into power. It's about being prepared to tackle the tangible aspects of financial management by drawing from a well-rounded toolkit.

To further motivate and encourage action, testimonials from those who have successfully embarked on similar wealth-building journeys can serve as powerful evidence of what's possible. Hearing stories of individuals who have overcome financial difficulties and achieved prosperity through diligent application of the strategies outlined can provide readers with a sense of camaraderie and belief that they too can realize similar outcomes. Real-life examples highlight the transformative impact of disciplined financial practices and reinforce the notion that success is attainable.

For young professionals eager to escape the paycheck-to-paycheck cycle, adopting these strategies can fundamentally alter their financial trajectory. By focusing on building a secure financial future, they can challenge their current economic status and position themselves for long-term prosperity. Likewise, middle-aged individuals looking to plan for retirement can utilize these insights to ensure their savings and investments support a comfortable lifestyle in later years. Established entrepreneurs can explore recommendations for establishing multiple streams of income, effectively expanding their portfolio beyond primary business endeavors to secure financial health (Financial Knowledge and Decision-Making Skills, 2021).

A proactive and goal-oriented mindset, coupled with informed decision-making, sets the foundation for each audience segment to engage with the book's material meaningfully. By encouraging readers to view their financial journey as a dynamic and ongoing process, they are more likely to adapt to changes and seize opportunities with agility. This perspective allows them to evolve alongside economic trends, thereby maximizing their potential for achieving financial freedom.

The ultimate aim is to cultivate readiness and enthusiasm among readers to transfer theoretical understanding into practice. Financial education without execution is merely unrealized potential. Delving into the practical application of acquired knowledge prepares readers to face real-world scenarios with conviction. Confidence grows when individuals see firsthand the effects of their strategic efforts, whether through successful budgeting, wise investments, or sustainable spending habits. As these skills are honed and results become evident, the cycle of learning and implementing reinforces itself, propelling readers ever closer to their financial aspirations.

Final Thoughts

As we conclude this chapter, it's vital to recognize the diverse strategies that pave the way toward financial freedom. We've highlighted key approaches like effective budgeting, strategic investment diversification, and the wise management of debts—all essential for building a secure financial foundation. Whether you're just starting out or planning for new financial horizons, these tools are adaptable to personal circumstances, empowering you to design a future free from monetary constraints. This journey is about adopting habits that support informed decisions, leading you closer to sustaining economic stability and independence.

Furthermore, the actionable steps discussed here cater to varied life stages, whether you're a young professional breaking free from the paycheck-to-paycheck cycle, a middle-aged individual aligning your savings for retirement, or an entrepreneur exploring multiple income avenues. By embracing the mindset of continuous learning and adapting to changes, you gain the agility needed to thrive in evolving financial landscapes. The power of real-life success stories within this narrative reinforces that while the path may be challenging, it is indeed possible. With commitment and proactive effort, reaching your financial goals becomes not just an aspiration, but an achievable reality.

Reference List

Avoiding Common Financial Mistakes in Business . (2024). Thefundingfamily.com. https://www.thefundingfamily.com/blog/avoiding-common-financial-mistakes

Batsters, E., & Batsters, E. (2024, November 14). *Self Employed* . Self Employed. https://www.selfemployed.com/why-is-it-important-to-set-realistic-goals/

Financial knowledge and decision-making skills . (2021). Consumer Financial Protection Bureau. https://www.consumerfinance.gov/consumer-tools/educator-tools/youth-financial-education/learn/financial-knowledge-decision-making-skills/

GAVIN, M. (2020). *5 Ways Managers Can Use Finance to Make Better Decisions | HBS Online* . Business Insights - Blog. https://online.hbs.edu/blog/post/financial-decision-making

Prevo, L., Kremers, S., & Jansen, M. (2020, January 18). *Small Successes Make Big Wins: A Retrospective Case Study towards Community Engagement of Low-SES Families* . International Journal of Environmental Research and Public Health. https://doi.org/10.3390/ijerph17020612

Setting SMART Financial Goals . (2024, April 2). Www.desertfinancial.com. https://www.desertfinancial.com/en/learn/blog/financial-education/smart-goals

SMART goals for your financial plan . (2022, November 10). Schwab Brokerage. https://www.schwab.com/learn/story/smart-goals-your-financial-plan

vorecol.com. (2015). *What are the most common pitfalls in financial performance management, and how can they be avoided?* Vorecol.com. https://vorecol.com/blogs/blog-what-are-the-most-common-pitfalls-in-financial-performance-management-and-how-can-they-be-avoided-151780

www.ingramcontent.com/pod-product-compliance
Lightning Source LLC
Chambersburg PA
CBHW071537220526
45469CB00003B/817